SEEDS OF HOPE

SEEDS OF HOPE

A Henri Nouwen Reader

ROBERT DURBACK, Editor

BANTAM BOOKS

TORONTO • NEW YORK • LONDON • SYDNEY • AUCKLAND

SEEDS OF HOPE

A Bantam Book / March 1989

Library of Congress Cataloging-in-Publication Data

Nouwen, Henri J. M.
  Seeds of hope.

  Bibliography: p.
  Includes index.
  1. Meditations.   I. Durback, Robert.   II. Title.
BX2182.2.N6742   1989   242   88-28496
ISBN 0-553-05332-9

Published simultaneously in the United States and Canada

Bantam Books are published by Bantam Books, a division of Bantam Doubleday Dell Publishing Group, Inc. Its trademark, consisting of the words "Bantam Books" and the portrayal of a rooster, is Registered in U.S. Patent and Trademark Office and in other countries. Marca Registrada. Bantam Books, 666 Fifth Avenue, New York, New York 10103.

PRINTED IN THE UNITED STATES OF AMERICA

DH   0   9   8   7   6   5   4   3   2   1

Contents

Acknowledgments   ix

Introduction—Preparing the Ground   xv

     Henri Nouwen, The Person   xx

     Henri Nouwen, The Writer   xxviii

PART ONE
SEEDS OF HOPE: HUMAN HUNGERS

Breaking Ground   3

Our Restless, Busy Society   6

Words and Silence   8

Loneliness   12

Solitude   14

On the Possibility and Desirability
of Love   17

Intimacy and Sexuality   18

Celebrating Humanness   25

Celebrating Children   32

Celebrating Life   35

PART TWO
SPRINGS OF HOPE: HOLINESS AND HUMANNESS

Who Is the Lord to Whom I Pray?   41

From Magic to Faith   43

The Search for God   47

Preaching and Ministry   53
Holiness, Humanness, and Prayer   62
How Can I Pray?—Three Rules   69
God's Presence and God's Absence   74
The Spirit of St. Francis   82
Displacement   90
Career and Vocation   94

PART THREE
THE ROOTS OF HOPE: HUMAN DESTINY

Nature as Revelation   99
Advent: Waiting   101
Christmas at the Abbey   108
The Mother of Christ   110
The Face of Christ   112
The Body of Christ   116
The Agony of Christ   122
The Human Journey: Aging and Dying   128
The Last Hours of Christ   138
The Glory of Christ   142

PART FOUR
HOPE IN A NUCLEAR AGE

The Predicament of Humanity in a Nuclear Age   153
Apocalypse Now   157
Mysticism in a Nuclear Age   159
Thomas Merton on Gandhi
and Nonviolence   161
Ecstasy in a Nuclear Age   164
A Parable   166

The Task of Peacemaking   168

Resistance   174

Second Coming   180

Last Judgment   183

Epilogue—Adam's Story: The Peace That Is Not
of This World   191

Bibliography   206

Index   209

Printing History   214

Acknowledgments

Publishing a first book has given me a new appreciation of the meaning of the word *community*. When I opened the letter from Bantam Books asking me to take on the work of compiling a Henri Nouwen Reader, I was excited, but I was also uneasy. It would be impossible to do it all on my own.

As a full-time letter carrier in the postal service, I knew a realistic response depended first of all on finding a typist, one who would be willing to work hard.

Janet Orban, who lived on the mail route I served, had just completed a smaller assignment for me. To her I owe my first word of thanks. To her husband, Lou, and their two children, Adam and Rebecca, I owe my next word of appreciation for their hospitality in allowing me to interrupt their family life at all hours, day and night, with armfuls of books and stacks of paper. To Adam and Rebecca and to all the children on my mail route I dedicate in a special way the section in the book on "Celebrating Children."

Then there was the need for that elusive commodity: time. To my Station Manager, Josephine Walker, I owe special appreciation for her support, understanding, and full cooperation in creating space for extra days off needed to make deadlines. To her assistants, Dick Humphrey and Katie Mullinax, to

Cleveland Postmaster Reginald Martin, to Nancy Erickson and Bob Harrigan I owe thanks for the role each played in the chain of command needed to open the door to my acceptance of a publishing contract.

Russell Faist merits singular recognition and gratitude for his careful reading and professional editing of the manuscript before its release to the publisher. To Jeanne Koma, faithful friend who for years has been first reader of whatever I have written, a hearty thank you. Rich Heffern of *Praying* magazine offered help in tackling inclusive language problems. Maria Mack of Bantam Books and Connie Ellis, secretary to Henri Nouwen, kept communication lines open with my principal contacts. I am grateful to all of them.

One does not undertake a work of this nature without recruiting a network of prayer-support. Here I must express my gratitude to my family and friends, to Christian Aidan Carr and the monks of Mepkin Abbey, who for many years have offered me a home away from home, to John Eudes Bamberger and the monks of the Abbey of the Genesee, to Patricia Kelly and the Carmelite Sisters of Reno, and to Anita Wasserman, Annamae Dannes and the Carmelite Sisters of Cleveland.

I am grateful to Joe and Karen Janesz, to Sarah, Katie, and Laura for their sustaining friendship; to my co-workers and to the families I serve on my mail route who, by sharing with me their stories, some of them tragic, have helped me to internalize the message I have assembled on paper. I owe particular mention to my many friends from the community of St. Angela parish who have supported me with their prayers throughout my work on the book.

A special word of thanks must be reserved for Michelle Rapkin, my editor at Bantam Books, who has supported me so enthusiastically from the start and done an excellent job of moving the manuscript to publication.

Finally my heartfelt gratitude to Henri Nouwen for the trust he has placed in me, for the gift he has enabled me to share with his many readers, the gift of his life, broken and given, bread for our journey.

rd

October 4, 1988
Feast of St. Francis of Assisi

Scripture quotations sometimes include reference to specific versions. Most frequently cited is the Jerusalem Bible *(JB). Other versions include the Revised Standard Version (RSV) and the New American Bible (NAB). In several instances quotations from the Psalms are taken from* The Psalms: A New Translation, *England, The Grail, 1963.*

A Note on Terminology: Nouwen's earlier works do not reflect his later sensitivity to the important issue of inclusive language. To bring the earlier texts up-to-date, I have, with the permission of the author and his publishers, made whatever revisions seemed appropriate to bring the text into conformity with inclusive standards.

INTRODUCTION

Preparing the Ground

When I was approached by Bantam Books to compile a selection of choice passages from Henri Nouwen, the theme of hope suggested itself at once as the unifying principle to bind the collection together. I was never tempted to abandon it in favor of another. If Nouwen has a single consistent message, it is a message of hope for a despairing world.

What is hope? Let me attempt an unorthodox definition of my own, formulated to explain in the simplest terms the theme I have chosen for the readings:

Hope is the inner dynamic that compels us to explore and pursue the expectations built into the human condition.

Hope was born the day the first human beings discovered the first bridge and decided not to jump off the bridge in despair, but to cross it.

These are not Henri Nouwen's words; they are my own. But they provide a point of departure for probing more deeply into the development of Nouwen's thought.

The book is divided into four sections:

Part I. Seeds of Hope: Human Hungers
Part II. Springs of Hope: Holiness and Humanness
Part III. The Roots of Hope: Human Destiny
Part IV. Hope in a Nuclear Age

PART I. SEEDS OF HOPE:
HUMAN HUNGERS

The implication clearly intended here is: our very human hungers are themselves seeds of hope. To be human is to be structured to hope. Let me refer again briefly to the picture of the first humans standing at the foot of the first bridge spanning an enormous chasm, joining a well known world to a world yet known.

Should they cross the bridge? Or should they play it safe and turn around and go back? There might be trouble on the other side. But then, there may also be new opportunity. Human hungers come into play. Yes, there is a risk involved if they cross over. But what might they miss if they turn around and go back? Human hunger wins out. Bridges are made to be crossed.

There, in very elemental form, are the basic components of hope as Nouwen lists them in his book, *With Open Hands*.

Hope expects the coming of something *new*.
Hope looks ahead toward that which is *not yet*.
Hope accepts and risks the *unspecified* (emphasis my own).

He quotes a student: "I see hope as an attitude where everything stays open before me. . . . Daring to stay open to whatever today will offer, or tomorrow . . . that is hope. To go fearlessly into things without knowing how they'll turn out; to keep on going even when something doesn't work the first time, to have trust in what you're doing."

Our human hungers, whether they be our craving for food, for intimacy, for adventure, for knowledge, for justice, for self-preservation, for ultimate survival beyond death—all these hungers are themselves deep forces embedded within our very nature pushing up the first green shoots from the seed of hope. This level of hope I would call "primordial hope," something planted very deeply in our flesh and bone, our psyche.

PART II. SPRINGS OF HOPE: HOLINESS AND HUMANNESS

Here we move to a level of hope that lifts us beyond our merely human capabilities: the realm of prayer and experience of a power beyond us. Nouwen describes this level of hope in *The Wounded Healer*:

> This hope stretches far beyond the limitations of one's own psychological strength, for it is anchored not just in the soul of the individual but in *God's self-disclosure in history.* (Emphasis my own)

Once we have spoken of reliance on a power beyond us, we are ready to move into a discussion of the nature of prayer.

Nouwen points out that traditionally we've divided prayer into four kinds: prayer of petition, adoration, praise, and thanksgiving. But he questions whether this fourfold distinction helps us understand what prayer is:

> The important thing about prayer is not whether it is classified as petition, thanksgiving, or praise, but whether it is a prayer of hope or of little faith.

He spells out the difference between the two:

> The prayer of little faith is filled with wishes which beg for immediate fulfillment. . . . With this prayer of little faith, it is the *concreteness* of the wishes which *eliminates the possibility for hope.* . . . Your spiritual life is reduced to a beeline toward what you want. (Emphasis my own)

The result of this kind of prayer:

> Because we are so eager to arrange for our own future, we of little faith close ourselves off from what, in fact, might be coming. . . . We become midgets in a world of tiny things. (*With Open Hands*)

With the prayer of little faith he contrasts the prayer of hope:

> When we live with hope we do not get tangled up with concerns for how our wishes will be fulfilled . . . ultimately it is not a question of having a wish come true but of expressing an unlimited faith in the giver of all good things. . . . For the prayer of hope, it is essential that there are no guarantees asked, no conditions posed, and no proofs demanded, only that you expect everything from the other without binding the other in any way.

He concludes:

> Only if you pray with hope can you break through the barriers of death. For no longer do you want to know what it will be like after you die, what heaven exactly will mean, how you will be eternal, or how the risen Lord will show himself. . . . When you pray with hope, you turn yourself toward a God who can be trusted unconditionally; it is enough to know that God is a faithful God.

The question can now be raised: Why should we trust so unhesitatingly in this God of promises? What basis is there for eliciting from us such unquestioning loyalty? These questions provide us with the opportunity to move on to the third division of the book.

PART III. THE ROOTS OF HOPE:
HUMAN DESTINY

Part Three deals predominantly with the third level of hope, which I would designate as specifically *Christian hope*. In the readings selected the emphasis will be on the mystery of Christ, the prototype and exemplar of what it means to be fully human. Gazing intently on the life, passion, death, and destiny of Jesus of Nazareth, Word made flesh, we glimpse the grandeur of the human destiny of us all. Christ is par excellence the Person of Hope who trusted unconditionally the one from whom he came.

Nouwen locates this third level of hope:

> . . . It is grounded in the historic Christ-event which is understood as a definitive breach in the deterministic chain of human trial and error, and as a dramatic affirmation that there is light on the other side of darkness. . . . Christ, who entered death with nothing but bare hope. (*The Wounded Healer*)

PART IV.
HOPE IN A NUCLEAR AGE

Part Four addresses specific contemporary issues that challenge all traditional formulations of faith. Here the hope we have spoken of is put to the ultimate test at each and every level. And yet the same basic guiding principles apply. We would like a concrete solution, a specific solution, and we would like it right now. Should we jump off the bridge that leads us into the year 2000? Or should we go forward and cross it? Nouwen urges us onward but cautions us to prepare ourselves for a journey which will require that we burn our bridges behind us.

To sum up: I have categorized hope under three levels:

1. Primordial hope: the hope that is "built into" our very humanity
2. Hope that reaches out beyond ourselves to a power beyond us
3. Specifically Christian hope, hope which flowers out of the mystery of Christ

Nouwen ties it all together:

> . . . Everything we are given and everything we are deprived of is nothing but a finger pointing out the direction of God's

hidden promise which we shall taste in full. (*With Open Hands*)

So much for the structure of the book. Before proceeding further with the reading selections, a brief biographical sketch of Henri Nouwen may provide a useful setting.

1
HENRI NOUWEN, THE PERSON

Who is Henri Nouwen? As I approach the task of painting the first strokes of a character sketch, I am aware of the author's sobering warning: "The mystery of one man is too immense and too profound to be explained by another man." (*The Wounded Healer*) Biographers beware.

I take heart, nonetheless, from the author's later observation: "Writing is like giving away the few loaves and fishes one has, trusting that they will multiply in the giving." ("Reflections on Theological Education")

Since the publication of his first book in 1969, Henri Nouwen has become one of the most sought-after figures both nationally and internationally, as lecturer, writer, keynote speaker, university professor, pastoral counselor, spiritual guide, and friend.

How does one explain his far-reaching appeal? My niece provided a good clue when she volunteered her spontaneous response at age seventeen after listening to one of his tapes: "It sounded as if he were reading my own heart." I think that response echoes the spoken or unspoken response of countless others who have found in Nouwen the "something more" they have been looking for. He has a way of searching out the hidden corners of his own soul, of openly and honestly sharing his personal struggles and vulnerabilities, which makes it easy for his listeners and readers to identify with him.

The following is a good description of his own style: "Christian leaders are . . . first of all, those who are willing to put their own articulated faith at the disposal of those who ask their help." (*The Wounded Healer*)

And again: "Ministry means the ongoing attempt to put one's own search for God, with all the moments of pain and joy, despair and hope, at the disposal of those who want to join this search but do not know how." (*Creative Ministry*) It is this quality of openly sharing his life with others that makes his ministry so extraordinary.

Henri Nouwen was born on January 24, 1932, the oldest of three brothers and one sister, in the small village of Nijkerk, about twenty-eight miles southeast of Amsterdam in Holland. By the time he was of school age, one of his first lessons would be in observing the skill of his parents and grandparents in hiding from the occupying forces of Germany. Because of the war his grandparents had moved in with the family.

He vividly recalls the harrowing incident after D-day when German soldiers forced their way into his parents' home, seeking to take his father into forced labor. His father, Laurent, knowing the danger that surrounded him daily, had carved out a well-concealed hiding place under a windowsill in a room in the attic. He remained there, in hiding, for entire days, reading by candlelight, always in suspense over a possible sudden incursion by Nazi soldiers, never certain whose footsteps he heard outside his hiding place. When soldiers finally did make their way into the home, there was no way of signaling to him to stay concealed where he was. When he heard the accustomed footsteps outside his hiding place under the windowsill, he was about to emerge to take the food he thought his father was bringing him but wisely followed his instinct that told him to remain silent until spoken to. The soldiers looked carefully around the room, found no one, and left the house. His obedience to his instinct saved him from captivity.

Though the war was disruptive in many ways, Maria Nouwen was determined that her son's schooling would not be interrupted. She convinced a small group of young Crozier Fathers of the wisdom of starting a school of their own in the neighboring village of Bussum, and Henri, with six other classmates, was able to continue his elementary education without interruption.

Nouwen recalls the war years not only as hard years but also as years filled with warm memories. While he remembers the scarcity of food and long, tiring bike rides to the country to obtain potatoes and other food from friends on a farm, he also remembers the years of growth and creativity.

As there was little opportunity for entertainment outside the home, his father was careful to organize cultural gatherings, inviting friends to come together to read poetry and to share paintings and other works of art. For the young Nouwen it was a time to be remembered for making many new friends, forging intimate bonds, and growing in appreciation of the experience of close community, rich in diversity with people from many different cultural and religious backgrounds.

By the time he was eighteen he was ready to enter the seminary. After one year in the minor seminary where his uncle was president, he went on to the major seminary in Utrecht, where he remained from 1951 until ordination in 1957. He describes himself during his student days as "never a good or a bright student, but a hardworking student." The good grades he received in his later seminary years he attributes not to brilliance but to determination, and "because I worked so crazy hard."

The seminary years were happy years. That he was very popular with his fellow students is evidenced by the fact that he was chosen to be "senior" or president of the entire student body. He insists that scholarship as such held little appeal for him. The focus of his interest was, from the beginning, and was to remain, *pastoral*, which is to say people- or person-oriented. He reflects: "It is unbelievable I ever made it to Yale! My presence on the faculty was more that of a pastor or a minister than a scholar. They knew that and accepted me that way."

Upon completion of his seminary studies, Nouwen was asked

by his bishop, later to be known as Bernard Cardinal Alfrink, to study theology. He asked the bishop if he would reconsider and allow him instead to major in psychology. The request was granted, and Nouwen resumed his studies at the University of Nijmegen, where he stayed from 1957 to 1964. During this period he made the first of many trips to the United States as chaplain on the Holland-America line and eventually began to explore the possibility of pursuing studies in psychology at Harvard under Gordon Allport. Allport convinced him that given the nature of his interest in psychology, he would do better to complete his studies at Nijmegen and then take advantage of an excellent program in psychiatry and religion offered at the Menninger Clinic in Topeka, Kansas.

Nouwen went on to Menninger, where he remained from 1964 to 1966, involving himself in clinical-pastoral education, research, and writing. There he made friends with Dr. John Santos, who opened yet another door. Santos was invited to begin a psychology department at the University of Notre Dame. Santos invited Nouwen to join him, asking him to teach two semesters at the university. Nouwen agreed, but upon the insistence of Father Theodore Hesburgh, the president, that he remain longer, extended his stay from 1966 to 1968.

Nouwen liked Notre Dame. He quickly made friends and forged relationships that would be long lasting. But he also began to see clearly that he would not be happy simply as a psychologist. His attention was drawn to the area of priestly formation and ministry. In 1968 he returned to Holland for a three-year stay. During the first two years he taught pastoral psychology and spirituality to students preparing themselves for the ordained ministry. His third year he spent working for a degree in theology at the University of Nijmegen.

In 1970 he received a letter which was to move him in yet another direction. The letter was from Yale University inviting him to come for a visit. He accepted the invitation, not suspecting that upon arrival he would be interviewed and pressed to join the faculty. Attractive though the offer was, Nouwen politely turned it down, affirming his commitment to the church in Holland. The issue was settled once and for all. Or so it seemed.

Six months later there was another letter asking him to reconsider and to accept a position on the faculty at Yale. He returned to Yale for a second visit and was impressed by the caliber and healthy mix of students from many different denominations. This time he accepted the teaching position with the approval of his bishop in Holland. He was to remain at Yale from 1971 to 1981, first as associate professor, and eventually as full professor of pastoral theology with tenure.

While based at Yale, he was able to also spend a semester at the Institute for Ecumenical and Cultural Research at St. John's University in Collegeville, Minnesota, and later at the Gregorian University and the North American College in Rome.

Of particular significance during the Yale years were two sabbaticals spent by special arrangement in a Trappist monastery in upstate New York. As a result of his close friendship with the abbot, Dom John Eudes Bamberger, Nouwen was given the unusual opportunity to live as an integrated though temporary member of the monastic community of the Abbey of the Genesee. From this period came two important works, *Genesee Diary* and *A Cry for Mercy*, of which more will be said later.

Nouwen was happy at Yale, but there were other fires burning inside him. A long-standing interest in the affairs of Latin America, which kept him commuting between two continents, reached a point where he felt compelled to respond to an inner voice calling him to give up his prestigious position on the faculty at Yale and to live, at least for a time, among the poor in the barrios of Lima, Peru.

In July 1981 he submitted his resignation from his tenured

position at Yale and began preparations, through his contacts with Maryknoll missioners, to spend six months in Bolivia and Peru. Three months were devoted to improving his Spanish by study in Bolivia, and for the remaining three months he worked as a missionary "in the field" among the poor of Peru. His immediate intent: to discern the answer to the question, "Does God call me to live and work in Latin America in the years to come?" Out of this period emerged *Gracias! A Latin American Journal.*

Nouwen did not opt to become a permanent resident of Latin America, but the picture he paints and the questions he raises in the journal recording his impressions during his six-month stay make informative, challenging reading especially for readers accustomed to the amenities of "first world" living standards.

In March 1982 he returned to the United States and took up residency in private living quarters made available for him on the grounds of Genesee Abbey. Shortly thereafter, letters began arriving from Harvard asking him to consider taking a position on the faculty there. He responded that he no longer wished to teach full-time at the university level. After many exchanges a compromise was reached which culminated in an agreement that he would teach only one semester a year at Harvard and be free for the second half of the year to pursue his other interests.

Nouwen moved to Cambridge in the late fall to prepare for his first teaching semester at Harvard in January 1983. When the semester ended he embarked again on another tour of Latin America, traveling first to Mexico, where he stayed for a month. While in Mexico he received an invitation from a Maryknoll missioner to visit Nicaragua. He accepted and soon found himself in the highly dangerous militarized zone on the border between Nicaragua and Honduras, meeting with peasants, listening to their stories, praying with them, and promising them he would return to the United States to tell his fellow North

Americans what he had heard and seen of the hardships and agony of his brothers and sisters south of the border.

He did not delay in keeping his promise but promptly returned to the United States to launch an extensive six-week lecture tour, during which he delivered impassioned accounts of the plight of war-torn, persecuted Nicaraguans and Hondurans, often wounded and put to death by weapons made and sent by the United States government. Segments of these lectures are found in this Reader.

Following his tour, Nouwen received an invitation to visit Jean Vanier, founder of the l'Arche community for the mentally handicapped in France. Nouwen welcomed the invitation and stayed six weeks. He was to return in the fall of the following year to make a thirty-day retreat under the direction of French Jesuit Père André de Jaer. The two visits were to mark another turning point in his spiritual journey.

Jean Vanier, founder of l'Arche, had been a professor of philosophy at St. Michael's College in Toronto when, in 1964, with the encouragement of his spiritual director, Père Thomas Philippe, a Dominican, he made the decision to leave the academic world and invited two mentally handicapped men to move into his home to form a household with him. It was not long before others, hearing of his move, asked to join him. Soon more households were formed. Eventually, volunteers began arriving from other countries, offering to come and live as assistants to the handicapped and to share their skills in various crafts. A new movement was born.

As of this writing, l'Arche constitutes an international federation numbering some eighty communities spread throughout such diverse countries as France, Britain, Ireland, Italy, Spain, Belgium, Switzerland, Denmark, India, Australia, the Ivory Coast, Burkina Fasso, the West Bank, Haiti, Honduras, Mexico, the Dominican Republic, Brazil, Canada, and the U.S.

In January 1985 Nouwen returned to his post at Harvard for

his third semester but found it increasingly difficult to remain in a purely academic environment. He sensed that his own spiritual life was in danger, and within weeks of semester's end he submitted his resignation.

Not long after that he wrote in his journal:

After only a few weeks away from the competitive, career-oriented life at Harvard Divinity School . . . I want to cry out loudly to my colleagues and students: "Do not serve Harvard, but God and his beloved Jesus Christ, and speak words of hope to those who suffer from loneliness, depression, and spiritual poverty." *But I myself have come to the painful discovery that when I am chained by ambition it is hard for me to see those who are chained by poverty. Therefore this is not a time to play the prophet, but a time to listen more carefully to the voice of God calling within me. *(Unpublished)

Soon after Nouwen had left Harvard he was invited by Jean Vanier to return to l'Arche in France for a longer stay, this time suggesting the possibility that he come to stay for a year. Nouwen received the invitation as a call from God. He was ready to respond. By late August he was aboard a jet, headed once again for France.

From August 1985 to August 1986 Nouwen familiarized himself with the world of the handicapped, eating with them, playing with them, working with them, and, above all, learning from them. What he learned he committed to writing. From this period emerged a new journal: *The Road to Daybreak: A Spiritual Journal.*

Daybreak is a family branch of l'Arche, founded in 1969 in Toronto. Inevitably, his involvement with l'Arche led Nouwen to a brief visit with the Daybreak community. It was not long after his visit that he received a letter inviting him to join the community at Daybreak on a long-term basis upon completion of his year at l'Arche. Nouwen again discerned a further call from God. With the approval of his cardinal archbishop in

Holland he accepted the invitation and pledged himself to a three-year commitment serving the Daybreak community, where he continues his ministry to the mentally handicapped today.

2
HENRI NOUWEN, THE WRITER

One might wonder how the fast-paced and well-traveled Nouwen found time to do any writing. There is ample evidence that he did indeed find time to write.

It is important, nevertheless, to point out from the start that before he is a writer, Nouwen is a speaker. His writing career began almost as an embarrassing accident. He had been asked to give a lecture to a conference of priests at the University of Notre Dame in the late sixties. After the lecture he was approached by a writer from the *National Catholic Reporter*. The reporter asked Nouwen for a copy of the lecture; Nouwen made one available, and it was rushed into print. The response was overwhelming. More articles were solicited, and Nouwen accommodated. His literary career was off the launch pad, and by 1969 a collection of the articles was put between two covers and published under the title *Intimacy*. A copy eventually landed on the desk of Colin Williams, dean of Yale. From that moment on Nouwen was targeted for recruitment to the faculty of the Yale Divinity School.

It is important to remember that Nouwen regards his writing as secondary to his teaching, preaching, and lecturing. Of the twenty-two books he has published to date, only one can claim its origin as the author's intent to "sit down and write a book." *Making All Things New* is the only book specifically undertaken at the previous request of a publisher. All the others "evolved" into books after much editing and rewriting. With the exception of his journals, most of his writings are the by-products of his lectures. First the spoken word. Then the book.

There are significant implications flowing from this. There is an immediacy and intensity in the spoken word that cannot be conveyed by the written word. One can produce the transcript of a lecture. But one cannot reproduce in writing the inflections, the emotion, the body language of the living word. The closer one gets to the living word, the closer one gets to the vital source with its power to move.

One has not "heard" Henri Nouwen until one has heard him speak. To provide the reader with the opportunity to hear at least a sampling of the live Nouwen on tape, a list of Nouwen's tapes has been compiled at the end of this book.

Having put Nouwen's writing and lecturing in their proper perspective, we are ready to move one step further. Ultimately, the lecturing and writing is the record of an intense search. All the rest is overflow. Education, scholarship, degrees—all have their place—but all are secondary to the Search. For what does he search? Everything within and just beyond reach: God, himself, the people and the world around him. Nothing is unimportant. To live is to search. And to follow the search wherever it takes you.

The starting point for this search is always his own heart: ". . . My lonely self . . . should be my first source of search and research." (*Reaching Out*) He goes on to say, "By slowly converting our loneliness into a deep solitude, we create that precious space where we can discover the voice telling us about our inner necessity—that is, our vocation." (*Ibid.*) *Vocation* is a key word in the Nouwen vocabulary. Closely related to it is the word *obedience*. Vocation has its root in the Latin word meaning "to call." Obedience springs from another Latin word meaning "to hear, to listen." The simple Latin root is the verb *audire*. The prefix "ob" added to it (*ob-audire*) signifies *intent* listening, keeping one's ear cupped so as to be sure not to miss a sound or syllable. Following one's "vocation," then, is listening intently to the voice of God calling. And being ready to leave everything behind to follow that call if need be.

How does one "pick up" the voice of God? In the Judeo-Christian tradition a special importance is attached to a faithful, prayerful reading of the Scriptures. By opening the Scriptures we expose ourselves, make ourselves available to the word of God as it addresses us personally and as members of the human community. This word, in the terms of the Letter to the Hebrews, is "living and active, sharper than any two-edged sword, piercing to the division of soul and spirit, of joints and marrow, and discerning the thoughts and intentions of the heart." (Heb. 4, 12, *RSV*)

Nouwen listens carefully to this word, allowing it to descend slowly from his mind into his heart, where it can speak to his innermost self and invite a response. A careful attention to the prominence given to the Scriptures in Nouwen's writings provides the reader with a focal point that makes for fruitful study.

Nouwen's writings are basically the record of his search to follow his own vocation, that is, the voice he listens for in the silence of his heart, the voice of God calling. By sharing in Nouwen's search, readers are, by implication, invited to explore their own hearts to see if there are any connecting points that might reveal where God is calling them.

A good place to begin is not with the first book published by Nouwen, but with the eighth, *Reaching Out*, published in 1975. This book is the centerpiece of all that the author has written to date. Everything published before leads up to it and all that follows flows from it. Nouwen gives his own evaluation in the introduction: ". . . Closer to me than anything I have written and tries to articulate my most personal thoughts and feelings about being a Christian."

In it, he traces three movements of the spiritual life: from loneliness to solitude, from hostility to hospitality, from illusion to prayer. These three themes are like three sluice gates that direct the flow of thought as Nouwen develops his reflection over the years to follow. Readers will profit by being alert to the emergence of these themes as they move from work to work in the Nouwen collection.

Sharing a common link with *Reaching Out* are four more books: *Intimacy, Creative Ministry, The Wounded Healer,* and *Aging*. Each traces its origin to lectures given at Notre Dame. *The Wounded Healer* deserves special mention as a carefully crafted, finely honed articulation of the author's probing vision of the new role and self-understanding required of the Christian leader in a nuclear age.

While these and many other of Nouwen's later works deal to a greater or lesser extent with the subject of pastoral ministry, the insights on which they draw have a broad-ranging appeal to anyone interested in the dynamics of spiritual growth, especially in the context of a fast-changing technological society. In Nouwen's thought, spirituality is not sharply divided between a clerical and a lay spirituality.

He notes in *Creative Ministry*: ". . . Every Christian is a minister." And again: ". . . What is true for ministers and priests in the formal sense is true for every man and woman who want to live their life in the light of the Gospel of Jesus Christ."

And in *The Wounded Healer*: "There is hardly a man or woman who does not exercise some leadership over other men or women." The Christian is by definition a person for others.

Aging raises the question: "Is aging a way to the darkness or a way to the light?" He explores how "the elderly are our teachers who tell us about the dangers as well as the possibilities in becoming old." A very powerful message on tape is available under the title "Aging and Ministry." (Ave Maria)

Thomas Merton: Contemplative Critic is the only book in which Nouwen makes a study of a single individual writer. But in this case the writer happens to be one of the most celebrated of the century. It is a good capsule introduction to the prolific Merton.

The best-selling Nouwen book, *With Open Hands*, is now in its seventeenth printing since its publication in 1972. Its popularity is easy to assess: an attractive format—short and enhanced with seventy-two full-page photos—on a single topic: prayer.

In the same category of general interest and popular readership are *Out of Solitude*, three short meditations on the Christian life, and *Making All Things New*, another pocket-size volume exploring the basics of Christian spirituality.

More specialized in their treatment of various aspects of

ministry and spirituality are *The Living Reminder, Clowning in Rome,* and *The Way of the Heart. Compassion,* while it may be included in this group, must be singled out for its exceptional depth, lengthier treatment, and careful preparation—five years in the making.

Two books deserve a "category" of their own. These are two deeply personal responses to Nouwen's mother's death after a brief illness in October 1978. *In Memoriam* gives a moving account of his experience of his mother's last days and hours. *A Letter of Consolation,* written from his retreat in a Trappist monastery, makes public a personal letter originally written to comfort his father in his bereavement. Readers will find in both books healing gifts to be shared with friends who have lost a loved one.

Three journals in the Nouwen collection call for more detailed comment. First in chronological order is *Genesee Diary,* already referred to in the biographical sketch. In the early sixties, while traveling from Miami to Topeka, Nouwen decided to make a visit to the Trappist Abbey of Gethsemani in Kentucky in the hope of finding someone with whom he could talk and share his personal concerns. When, upon arrival, he mentioned his work as a psychologist, he was quickly introduced to Father John Eudes Bamberger, one of the monks, a physician specializing in psychiatry. The relationship clicked. A new and lasting friendship was begun.

Several years later John Eudes was elected abbot of the Abbey of the Genesee in upstate New York. The stage was set for the fulfillment of a dream that had since taken shape in Nouwen's mind. He broached the question of the possibility of his making an extended stay at the abbey as a "temporary monk" during a sabbatical from his teaching position at Yale. The abbot pointed out that such a request was not normally granted, but he promised he would discuss it with the monks to see if an exception could be made.

Six months later Nouwen got the good news: The monks had

"voted him in"! On June 1, 1974, Nouwen arrived at the abbey gate, and on June 2, Pentecost Sunday, he wrote the first page of what would become *Genesee Diary: Report from a Trappist Monastery.*

A special treat offered by the diary is the opportunity to eavesdrop on the conversations of two masters of the spiritual life as the author shares his honest self-disclosure with John Eudes, his friend and spiritual guide.

A companion to *Genesee Diary* is *A Cry for Mercy: Prayers from the Genesee.* Nouwen found his seven-month stay at the abbey a unique opportunity to reassess his own life as a busy lecturer, writer, and university professor in the context of the slower-paced lifestyle of the monks. When the opportunity came up again five years later, he asked if he could return for a second stay of seven months. This time he lived a new experiment: He wrote a prayer each day. It is difficult to read these prayers without at some point hearing the cry from one's own heart.

The second of Nouwen's journals, *Gracias! A Latin American Journal,* was mentioned earlier. In an article published in *America* (April 21, 1984), Nouwen provides an insight into the inner convictions that finally led to his decision to resign from his post on the faculty at Yale in 1981. In the article he states:

> When I came to the United States in 1971, not for a visit, a course, or a sabbatical, but to make my home here, I had an intuition that would grow stronger as the years went by. It was the intuition that the spiritual destiny of North America is intimately linked to the spiritual destiny of South America. Somehow I sensed that in order to come to know the living Christ among the people in the northern part of the Americas I had to be willing to expose myself to the way the living Christ reveals himself in the southern part of the Americas.

Gracias! is a chronicle of that self-chosen exposure. In it the reader is challenged repeatedly to recognize that "the tragic political, economic, and military events that we are living today

are the symptoms of a spiritual event of which we are part."
(*America*, 1984)

Somewhat related to *Gracias!* is a smaller book which followed two years later. *Love in a Fearful Land: A Guatemalan Story* is
the story of two priests in Guatemala. The first, Father Stanley
Francis Rother, was murdered in 1982 while serving his people
in Santiago Atitlan. The second, Father John Vesey, a friend of
Nouwen's, provides a rare on-site report of the risks involved in
being successor to a martyred priest three years later. More than
just the story of two priests, *Love in a Fearful Land* is a consciousness-
raising first-hand account of a people of faith struggling against
enormous odds in the face of government persecution and
intrigue.

Lifesigns marks a new phase in the Nouwen journey: the
transition from the university to ministry among the mentally
handicapped. Nouwen credits Jean Vanier with the idea for the
three themes expressed in the subtitle: *Intimacy, Fecundity, and
Ecstasy in Christian Perspective.* Written for the greater part during
visits to l'Arche, *Lifesigns* addresses a phenomenon particularly
symptomatic of our time: "The agenda of our world . . . is an
agenda of fear and power." Noting how easily we make this
agenda our own, he turns to St. John, who states in his first
letter that "perfect love casts out all fear." Weaving his thought
around the familiar concepts of intimacy, fecundity, and ecstasy, Nouwen reveals the possibility of "a movement from the
house of fear to the house of love."

A later volume coming under the influence of Nouwen's
interest in working with the mentally handicapped is *Behold the
Beauty of the Lord: Praying with Icons.* On his first visit to l'Arche a
copy of Rublev's icon of the Trinity was placed on the table of
the room in which he was staying. After prayerfully gazing on it
for many weeks, his writer's urge could no longer be contained.
During a second visit another icon was placed before him, the
icon of Our Lady of Vladimir. Once again he took up his pen.
A third visit found him reflecting on Rublev's "Savior of

Zvenigorod," and a fifteenth-century Russian icon, "The Descent of the Holy Spirit." The reader is invited to join the author in his reflection and to "behold the beauty of the Lord." Fold-out reproductions of the four icons are provided in the book.

The Road to Daybreak marks Nouwen's third journal and the most recent of his books to date. Here we get a close-up of his new ministry to the mentally handicapped. We meet Michael, severely afflicted with epilepsy, who wants to help him celebrate Mass and wear a red stole as he does. We meet Janice, Carol, Adam, and Rose and discover the patience and care required to help them pick apples: "My attitude was to get the apples picked, put them in bags, and go home. But I soon learned that all of that was much less important than to help Rose pick one or two apples, to walk with Janice and Carol looking for apples that hung low enough so that they themselves could reach them . . . and just to sit with Adam in his wheelchair under an apple tree and give him a sense of belonging to the group."

Seasoned with lively accounts of travels and comments on events mundane and holy as he commutes from Europe to Canada, and to the United States, *The Road to Daybreak* beckons the reader to join the author on his latest journey.

In October 1980, an honorary doctorate was conferred on Nouwen by Virginia Theological Seminary. The statement on the citation handed him reads in part:

For a generation of Christians in search of their lost humanity and a forgotten spirituality, you have found a way out of solitude into creative discipleship and ministry. Few of your contemporaries have managed with such grace and clarity to combine the insights of modern psychology with the ancient truths of biblical religion. As a pastoral theologian your own vital priesthood serves as a living reminder to your colleagues in ministry of the need to help each new generation hear and understand the loving compassion of the Word of God.

Through your books and essays, your published meditations and reflections, you have become one of the most widely read interpreters of the Christian way for seekers and followers in our time. And when you preach and teach the Gospel of God's renewing love in Christ, your hearers know the power of prophecy, evangelism, and the priestly cure of souls.

Born and bred in the old world, you are now at home in the new. Baptized and ordained by the Catholic Church, you are now at home in many traditions and communities of the Christian family. Though a university scholar and professor, you have discovered the secret of teaching all sorts and conditions of searching souls.

That sums up the impact Nouwen has had in the more than twenty years of his public ministry of the spoken and written word. In a particularly trenchant passage in *The Wounded Healer*, Nouwen paints a picture of authentic leadership that turns out to be a good self-portrait. It makes a fitting conclusion to this section:

> . . . Pastoral conversation is not merely a skillful use of conversational techniques to manipulate people into the Kingdom of God, but a deeper human encounter in which men and women are willing to put their own faith and doubt, their own hope and despair, their own light and darkness at the disposal of others who want to find a way through their confusion and touch the solid core of life. In this context, preaching means more than handing over a tradition; it is rather the careful and sensitive articulation of what is happening in the community so that those who listen can say: "You say what I suspected, you express what I vaguely felt, you bring to the fore what I fearfully kept in the back of my mind. Yes, yes—you say who we are, you recognize our condition. . . ."

That is Nouwen's gift to his readers. He tells us who we are. And to give a person or a community an identity is to plant the seed of hope.

I

SEEDS OF HOPE: HUMAN HUNGERS

*... I feel a growing desire to
enter into this world and to speak
a word of hope.*

–HENRI J. M. NOUWEN
Genesee Diary

Breaking Ground

1

Thinking back on how I came to the ideas I have written down on paper, I realize how much they were the result of a constant interaction with people. I write against the background of my own history and experiences and others respond to me from their different histories and experiences, and it is in the interaction of stories that the ideas take their shape.

Someone might read what I wrote and discover something there that I myself did not see but which might be just as valid as my original thought. It seems important to allow this to happen. If I were to try to prevent people from drawing "wrong" implications from my thoughts, I might fall into the temptation of thinking that I know what all the implications are. Maybe I should be happy that I do not know them. In this way, many people with quite different stories can move between the lines of my hesitant ideas, opinions, and viewpoints and there create their own. After all, people will never follow anyone's ideas except their own; I mean, those which have developed within their inner selves.

Genesee Diary

2

I wanted to write this book because it is my growing conviction that my life belongs to others just as much as it belongs to myself, and that what is experienced as most unique often proves to be most solidly embedded in the common condition of being human.

Reaching Out

3

When I went home last night, I thought, "What do I have to say to these men and women who are so earnest in their search for God and live such good lives?" But then I realized that the only thing I have to do is to say loudly what they already know in their hearts so that they can recognize it as really theirs and affirm it in gratitude.

Genesee Diary

4

This can be a true book for Christians only when it addresses itself also to those whose many questions about the meaning of life have remained open-ended. The authentic spiritual life finds its basis in the human condition, which all people—whether they are Christians or not—have in common.

Making All Things New

. . . Writing about the spiritual life is like making prints from negatives. . . . Often it is the dark forest that makes us speak about the open field. Frequently prison makes us think about freedom, hunger helps us to appreciate food, and war gives us words for peace. Not seldom are our visions of the future born out of the sufferings of the present and our hope for others out of our own despair. Only few "happy endings" make us happy, but often someone's careful and honest articulation of the ambiguities, uncertainties, and painful conditions of life gives us new hope. The paradox is indeed that new life is born out of the pains of the old.

Reaching Out

Our Restless,
Busy Society

MAY 13, 1986

What most strikes me, being back in the United States, is the full force of the restlessness, the loneliness, and the tension that holds so many people. The conversations I had today were about spiritual survival. So many of my friends feel overwhelmed by the many demands made on them; few feel the inner peace and joy they so much desire.

To celebrate life together, to be together in community, to simply enjoy the beauty of creation, the love of people and the goodness of God—those seem faraway ideals. There seems to be a mountain of obstacles preventing people from being where their hearts want to be. It is so painful to watch and experience. The astonishing thing is that the battle for survival has become so "normal" that few people really believe that it can be different. . . . I want so much to bring them to new places, show them new perspectives, and point out to them new ways. But in this hectic, pressured, competitive, exhausting context, who can really hear me? I even wonder how long I myself can stay in touch with the voice of the spirit when the demons of this world make so much noise.

Oh how important is discipline, community, prayer, silence, caring presence, simple listening, adoration, and deep, lasting faithful friendship. We all want it so much, and still the powers suggesting that all of that is fantasy are enormous. But we have to replace the battle for power with the battle to create space for the spirit.

The Road to Daybreak

Words and Silence

1

One of our main problems is that in this chatty society, silence has become a very fearful thing. For most people, silence creates itchiness and nervousness. Many experience silence not as full and rich, but as empty and hollow. For them silence is like a gaping abyss which can swallow them up. As soon as a minister says during a worship service "Let us be silent for a few moments," people tend to become restless and preoccupied with only one thought: "When will this be over?" Imposed silence often creates hostility and resentment. Many ministers who have experimented with silence in their services have soon found out that silence can be more demonic than divine and have quickly picked up the signals that were saying "Please keep talking." It is quite understandable that most forms of ministry avoid silence precisely so as to ward off the anxiety it provokes.

The Way of the Heart

2

Recently I was driving through Los Angeles, and suddenly I had the strange sensation of driving through a huge dictionary. Wherever I looked there were words trying to take my eyes from the road. They said, "Use me, take me, buy me, drink me, smell me, touch me, kiss me, sleep with me." In such a world, who can maintain respect for words?

All this is to suggest that words, my own included, have lost their creative power. Their limitless multiplication has made us lose confidence in words and caused us to think, more often than not, "They are just words."

Teachers speak to students for six, twelve, eighteen, and sometimes twenty-four years. But the students often emerge from the experience with the feeling: "They were just words." Preachers preach their sermons week after week and year after year. But their parishioners remain the same and often think: "They are just words." Politicians, businessmen, ayatollahs, and popes give speeches and make statements "in season and out of season," but those who listen say: "They are just words . . . just another distraction."

The result of this is that the main function of the word, which is communication, is no longer realized. The word no longer communicates, no longer fosters communion, no longer creates community, and therefore no longer gives life. The word no longer offers trustworthy ground on which people can meet each other and build society.

The Way of the Heart

3

Silence is the home of the word. Silence gives strength and fruitfulness to the word. We can even say that words are meant to disclose the mystery of the silence from which they come.

The Taoist philosopher Chuang Tzu expresses this well in the following way:

> The purpose of a fish trap is to catch fish and when the fish are caught, the trap is forgotten. The purpose of a rabbit snare is to catch rabbits. When the rabbits are caught, the snare is forgotten. The purpose of the word is to convey ideas. When the ideas are grasped, the words are forgotten. Where can I find a man who has forgotten words? He is the one I would like to talk to.[1]

The Way of the Heart

"I would like to talk to the man who has forgotten words." That could have been said by one of the Desert Fathers. For them, the word is the instrument of the present world and silence is the mystery of the future world. If a word is to bear fruit, it must be spoken from the future world into the present world. The Desert Fathers therefore considered their going into the silence of the desert to be a first step into the future world. From that world their words could bear fruit because there they could be filled with the power of God's silence.

The Way of the Heart

4

GOD'S SILENCE

Out of eternal silence God spoke the Word, and through this Word created and recreated the world. In the beginning God spoke the land, the sea, and the sky. God spoke the sun, the moon, and the stars. God spoke plants, birds, fish, animals wild and tame. Finally, God spoke man and woman. Then, in the fullness of time, God's Word, through whom all had been created, became flesh and gave power to all who believe to become the children of God. In all this, the Word of God does not break the silence of God, but rather unfolds the immeasurable richness of that silence. . . .

A word with power is a word that comes out of silence. A word that bears fruit is a word that emerges from the silence and returns to it.

The Way of the Heart

Loneliness

One way to express the spiritual crisis of our time is to say that most of us have an address but cannot be found there.

Making All Things New

1

Loneliness is one of the most universal sources of human suffering today. Psychiatrists and clinical psychologists speak about it as the most frequently expressed complaint and the root not only of an increasing number of suicides but also of alcoholism, drug use, different psychosomatic symptoms—such as headaches and stomach and low-back pains—and of a large number of traffic accidents. Children, adolescents, adults, and old people are in growing degree exposed to the contagious disease of loneliness in a world in which a competitive individualism tries to reconcile itself with a culture that speaks about togetherness, unity, and community as the ideals to strive for. . . .

The roots of loneliness are very deep and cannot be touched by optimistic advertisement, substitute love images, or social togetherness. They find their food in the suspicion that there is no one who cares and offers love without conditions, and no place where we can be vulnerable without being used.

Reaching Out

2

But what then can we do with our essential aloneness which so often breaks into our consciousness as the experience of a desperate sense of loneliness? What does it mean to say that neither friendship nor love, neither marriage nor community can take that loneliness away? Sometimes illusions are more livable than realities, and why not follow our desire to cry out in loneliness and search for someone whom we can embrace and in whose arms our tense body and mind can find a moment of deep rest and enjoy the momentary experience of being understood and accepted? These are hard questions because they come forth out of our wounded hearts, but they have to be listened to even when they lead to a difficult road. This difficult road is the road of conversion, the conversion from loneliness into solitude. Instead of running away from our loneliness and trying to forget or deny it, we have to protect it and turn it into a fruitful solitude. To live a spiritual life we must first find the courage to enter into the desert of our loneliness and to change it by gentle and persistent efforts into a garden of solitude. This requires not only courage but also a strong faith. As hard as it is to believe that the dry, desolate desert can yield endless varieties of flowers, it is equally hard to imagine that our loneliness is hiding unknown beauty. The movement from loneliness to solitude, however, is the beginning of any spiritual life because it is the movement from the restless senses to the restful spirit, from the outward-reaching cravings to the inward-reaching search, from the fearful clinging to the fearless play.

Reaching Out

Solitude

1

Solitude begins with a time and place for God, and God alone. If we really believe not only that God exists but also that God is actively present in our lives—healing, teaching, and guiding—we need to set aside a time and space to give God our undivided attention. Jesus says, "Go to your private room and, when you have shut your door, pray to your Father who is in that secret place" (Matt. 6:6).

To bring some solitude into our lives is one of the most necessary but also most difficult disciplines. Even though we may have a deep desire for real solitude, we also experience a certain apprehension as we approach that solitary place and time. As soon as we are alone, without people to talk with, books to read, TV to watch, or phone calls to make, an inner chaos opens up in us. This chaos can be so disturbing and so confusing that we can hardly wait to get busy again. Entering a private room and shutting the door, therefore, does not mean that we immediately shut out all our inner doubts, anxieties, fears, bad memories, unresolved conflicts, angry feelings, and impulsive desires. On the contrary, when we have removed our outer distractions, we often find that our inner distractions manifest themselves to us in full force. We often use the outer distractions to shield ourselves from the interior noises. It is thus not surprising that we have a difficult time being alone. The confrontation with our inner conflicts can be too painful for us to endure.

This makes the discipline of solitude all the more important.

Making All Things New

2

Solitude is not a spontaneous response to an occupied and preoccupied life. There are too many reasons not to be alone. Therefore we must begin by carefully planning some solitude. Five or ten minutes a day may be all we can tolerate. Perhaps we are ready for an hour every day, an afternoon every week, a day every month, or a week every year. The amount of time will vary for each person according to temperament, age, job, life-style, and maturity. But we do not take the spiritual life seriously if we do not set aside some time to be with, and listen to, God. We may have to write it in black and white in our daily calendar so that nobody else can take away this period of time.

Making All Things New

3

Once we have committed ourselves to spending time in solitude, we develop an attentiveness to God's voice in us. In the beginning, during the first days, weeks, or even months, we may have the feeling that we are simply wasting our time. Time in solitude may at first seem little more than a time in which we are bombarded by thousands of thoughts and feelings that emerge from hidden areas of our mind. One of the early Christian writers describes the first stage of solitary prayer as the experience of someone who, after years of living with open doors, suddenly decides to shut them. Visitors who used to come and enter the home start pounding on the doors, wondering why they are not allowed to enter. Only when they realize that they are not welcome do they gradually stop coming. This is the experience of anyone who decides to enter into solitude after a life without much spiritual discipline. At first, the many distractions keep presenting themselves. Later, as they receive less and less attention, they slowly withdraw.

Making All Things New

4

When we are not afraid to enter into our own center and to concentrate on the stirrings of our own soul, we come to know that being alive means being loved. This experience tells us that we can love only because we are born out of love, that we can give only because our life is a gift, and that we can make others free only because we are set free by God whose heart is greater than ours. When we have found the anchor places for our lives in our own center, we can be free to let others enter into the space created for them and allow them to dance their own dance, sing their own song, and speak their own language without fear. Then our presence is no longer threatening and demanding but inviting and liberating.

The Wounded Healer

On the Possibility and Desirability of Love

I would like to consider this as a report on the possibility and desirability of love. For the question is not, 'What should I do if I find myself in deep love with another stranger in this world?' but, rather, 'Can this love ever be a reality at all?' Many are asking themselves if we are doomed to remain strangers to each other. Is there a spark of misunderstanding in every intimate encounter, a painful experience of separateness in every attempt to unite, a fearful resistance in every act of surrender? Is there a fatal component of hate in the center of everything we call love?

We probably have wondered in our many lonesome moments if there is one corner in this competitive, demanding world where it is safe to be relaxed, to expose ourselves to someone else, and to give unconditionally. It might be very small and hidden. But if this corner exists, it calls for a search through the complexities of our human relationships in order to find it.

Intimacy

Intimacy and Sexuality

INTERPERSONAL RELATIONSHIPS

We can safely say that in the Western culture of the last few decades the value of coming together, being together, living together, and loving together has received more attention than ever before. The healing power of eye contact, of attentive listening, and of the careful touch has been explored by many psychologists, sensitivity trainers, and communication experts. Practically every year you can hear about a new type of therapy, a new form of consciousness enlarging, or a new method of communication. Many, many people suffering from feelings of isolation, alienation, or loneliness have found new hope and strength in these experiments in togetherness. Just seeing the great popularity and the growing influence of reevaluation therapy is enough to convince a sympathetic observer that a deep need is being responded to.

We indeed need each other and are able to give each other much more than we often realize. Too long have we been burdened by fear and guilt, and too long have we denied each other the affection and closeness we rightly desire. We, therefore, have much to learn from those who are trying to open up new and more creative interpersonal relations.

But critical questions still need to be raised. Can real intimacy be reached without a deep respect for that holy place within and between us, that space that should remain un-touched by human hands? Can human intimacy really be fulfill-ing when every space within and between us is being filled up? Is the emphasis on the healing possibilities of human together-ness not often the result of a one-sided perception of our human predicament? These questions have a new urgency in the time of the human potential movements.

I often wonder if we do not think or feel that our painful experiences of loneliness are primarily results of a lack of inter-personal closeness. We seem to think: "If I could just break through my fear to express my real feelings of love and hostil-ity, if I could just feel free to hold a friend, if I could just talk honestly and openly with my own people. If I could just live with someone who really cares . . . then I would have again some inner peace and experience again some inner wholeness." When any of these experiences have become reality to us we feel, in fact, a certain relief, but the question remains if it is there that the real source of our healing and wholeness can be found.

Clowning in Rome

A Suffocating Closeness

In a world in which traditional patterns of human communica-tions have broken down and in which family, profession, or village no longer offer the intimate bonds they did in the past, the basic human condition of aloneness has entered so deeply into our emotional awareness that we are constantly tempted to want more from our fellow human beings than they can give. If we relate to our neighbors with the supposition that they are able to fulfill our deepest needs, we will find ourselves increas-ingly frustrated, because, when we expect a friend or lover to be able to take away our deepest pain, we expect from him or her something that cannot be given by human beings. No human being can understand us fully, no human being can give us unconditional love, no human being can offer constant affection, no human being can enter into the core of our being and heal our deepest brokenness. When we forget that and expect from others more than they can give, we will be quickly disillusioned; for when we do not receive what we expect, we easily become resentful, bitter, revengeful, and even violent. . . .

Spinoza's words "Nature abhors a vacuum" seem quite applicable to us, and the temptation is indeed very great to take flight into an intimacy and closeness that does not leave any open space. Much suffering results from this suffocating closeness.

Clowning in Rome

WITH PRAYING HANDS

I found a good image to describe our predicament in the book *Existential Metapsychiatry* by New York psychiatrist Thomas Hora. . . . Hora calls the great emphasis on interpersonal relationships as the way to healing *personalism*, and he compares this personalism with the interlocking fingers of two hands. The fingers of the two hands can intertwine only to the point that a stalemate is reached. After that the only possible movement is backward, causing friction and eventually pain. And too much friction leads to separation. When we relate to each other as the interlocking fingers of two hands, we enter into a suffocating closeness that does not leave any free space. When lonely people with a strong desire for intimacy move closer and closer to each other in the hope of coming to an experience of belonging and wholeness, all too frequently they find themselves locked in a situation in which closeness leads to friction, friction to pain, and pain to separation.

Many marriages are so short-lived precisely because there is an intense desire for closeness and a minimal amount of space that allows for free movement. Because of the high emotional expectation with which they enter into a relationship, married couples often panic when they do not experience the inner contentment for which they had hoped. Often they try very hard to alleviate their tensions by exploring in much detail their life together, only to end up in a stalemate, tired, exhausted, and finally forced to separate in order to avoid mutual harm.

Hora suggests as the image for a true human relationship two hands coming together parallel in a prayerful gesture, pointing beyond themselves and moving freely in relation to each other. I find this a helpful image exactly because it makes it clear that a mature human intimacy requires a deep and profound respect for the free and empty space that needs to exist within and between partners and that asks for a continuous mutual protection and nurture. Only in this way can a relationship be lasting, precisely because mutual love is experienced as a participation in a greater and earlier love to which it points. In this way intimacy can be rich and fruitful, since it has been given carefully protected space in which to grow. This relationship no longer is a fearful clinging to each other but a free dance, allowing space in which we can move forward and backward, form constantly new patterns, and see each other as always new.

Clowning in Rome

A DWELLING PLACE FOR GOD

Marriage is not a lifelong attraction of two individuals to each other, but a call for two people to witness together to God's love. The basis of marriage is not mutual affection, or feelings, or emotions and passions that we associate with love, but a vocation, a being elected to build together a house for God in this world, to be like the two cherubs whose outstretched wings sheltered the Ark of the Covenant and created a space where Yahweh could be present (Ex. 25:10–12, 1 Kings 8:6–7). Marriage is a relationship in which a man and a woman protect and nurture the inner sanctum within and between them and witness to that by the way in which they love each other. . . . Celibacy is part of marriage not simply because married couples may have to be able to live separated from each other for long periods of time, or because they may need to abstain from sexual relations for physical, mental, or spiritual reasons, but also because the intimacy of marriage itself is an intimacy that is based on the common participation in a love greater than the love two people can offer each other.

The real mystery of marriage is not that husband and wife love each other so much that they can find God in each other's lives, but that God loves them so much that they can discover each other more and more as living reminders of God's presence. They are brought together, indeed, as two prayerful hands extended toward God and forming in this way a home for God in this world.

Clowning in Rome

LOVE ASKS
FOR TOTAL DISARMAMENT

Love asks for a total *disarmament*. The encounter in love is an encounter without weapons. Perhaps the disarmament in the individual encounter is more difficult than international disarmament. We are very able to hide our guns and knives even in the most intimate relationship. An old bitter memory, a slight suspicion about motives, or a small doubt can be as sharp as a knife held behind our back as a weapon for defense in case of attack. Can we ever meet a friend or stranger without any protection? Reveal ourselves to another in our total vulnerability? This is the heart of our question. Are man and woman able to exclude the power in their relationship and become totally available for each other? When the soldier sits down to eat he lays down his weapons because eating means peace and rest. When he stretches out his body to sleep he is more vulnerable than ever. Table and bed are the two places of intimacy where love can manifest itself in weakness. In love men and women take off all the forms of power, embracing each other in total disarmament. The nakedness of their bodies is only a symbol of total vulnerability and availability.

When the physical encounter of men and women in the intimate act of intercourse is not an expression of their total availability to each other, the creative fellowship of the weak is not yet reached. Every sexual relationship with built-in reservations, with mental restrictions, or time limits is still part of the taking structure. It means "I want you now but not tomorrow. I want something from you, but I don't want *you.*" Love is limitless. Only when men and women give themselves to each other in total surrender, that is, with their whole person for their whole life, can their encounter bear full fruits.

When through the careful growth of their relationship men and women have come to the freedom of total disarmament, their giving also becomes for-giving, their nakedness does not evoke shame but desire to share, and their ultimate vulnerability becomes the core of their mutual strength. New life is born in the state of total vulnerability—this is the mystery of love. Power kills. Weakness creates. It creates autonomy, self-awareness, and freedom. It creates openness to give and receive in mutuality. And finally it creates the good ground on which new life can come to full development and maturity. This explains why the highest safeguard for the physical, mental, and spiritual health of the child is not primarily the attention paid to the child but the unrestricted love of the parents for each other.

If the taking form of existence were the only possibility, destruction would be our fate. But if love can be found, creation can exist. Because love is based, as Merton says, on the belief in the reversibility of evil. Evil, then, is not final and unchangeable. Gandhi's concept of nonviolence was essentially based on his conviction that forgiveness could change every enemy into a friend, that in hatred love is hidden, in despair hope, in doubt faith, in evil good, in sin redemption. Love is an act of forgiving in which evil is converted to good and destruction into creation. In the truthful, tender, and disarmed encounter of love, we are able to create. In this perspective it becomes clear that the sexual act is a religious act. Out of the total disarmament of a man and a woman on their cross, exposing themselves in their extreme vulnerability, two new persons arise and manifest themselves in freedom. Is it not exactly in this same act of self-surrender that we find our highest fulfillment which expresses itself in the new life we create?

Religion and sexuality, which in the past have been so often described as opponents, merge into one and the same reality when they are seen as an expression of the total self-surrender in love.

Intimacy

If there is a need for a new morality it is the morality which teaches us the fellowship of the weak as a human possibility. Love, then, is not a clinging to each other in the fear of an oncoming disaster but an encounter in a freedom that allows for the creation of new life. This love cannot be proved. We can only be invited to it and find it to be true by an engaging response. As long as we experience the Christian life as a life which puts restrictions on our freedom of expression, we have perverted and inverted its essence.

Intimacy

Celebrating
Humanness

THE BIRDS AND I

GENESEE ABBEY, JUNE 13, 1974

This morning Father John explained to me that the killdeer is a bird that fools you by simulating injury to pull your attention away from her eggs which she lays openly on a sandy place. Beautiful! Neurosis as weapon! How often I have asked pity for a very unreal problem in order to pull people's attention away from what I didn't want them to see.

Sometimes it seems that every bird has institutionalized one of my defense mechanisms. The cowbird lays her eggs in some other bird's nest to let them do the brooding job; the Baltimore oriole imitates the sounds of more dangerous birds to keep the enemies away, and the redwing blackbird keeps screaming so loudly overhead that you get tired of her noise and soon leave the area that she considers hers. It does not take long to realize that I do all of that and a lot more to protect myself or to get my own will done.

Genesee Diary

FAILURE

The great temptation is to use our many obvious failures and disappointments in our lives to convince ourselves that we are really not worth being loved. Because what do we have to show for ourselves?

But for a person of faith the opposite is true. The many failures may open that place in us where we have nothing to brag about but everything to be loved for. It is becoming a child again, a child who is loved simply for being, simply for smiling, simply for reaching out.

This is the way to spiritual maturity: to receive love as a pure, free gift.

Unpublished journal

FORGIVENESS

NOVEMBER 11, 1985

This morning I meditated on God's eagerness to forgive me, revealed in the words of Psalm 103: "As far as the East is from the West so far does God remove my sin." In the midst of all my distractions, I was touched by God's desire to forgive me again and again. If I return to God with a repentant heart after I have sinned, God is always there to embrace me and let me start afresh. "The Lord is compassion and love, slow to anger, and rich in mercy."

It is hard for me to forgive someone who has really offended me, especially when it happens more than once. I begin to doubt the sincerity of the one who asks forgiveness for a second, third, or fourth time. But God does not keep count. God just waits for our return, without resentment or desire for revenge. God wants us home. "The love of the Lord is everlasting."

Maybe the reason it seems hard for me to forgive others is that I do not fully believe that I am a forgiven person. If I could fully accept the truth that I am forgiven and do not have to live in guilt or shame, I would really be free. My freedom would allow me to forgive others seventy times seven times. By not forgiving, I chain myself to a desire to get even, thereby losing my freedom. A forgiven person forgives. This is what we proclaim when we pray: ". . . And forgive us our trespasses as we forgive those who have trespassed against us."

This lifelong struggle lies at the heart of the Christian life.

The Road to Daybreak

ON WRITING

The written word has a very important place in our society. Even though radio and television have become major forms of communication, the written word continues to remain the most formative and influential way in which thoughts are expressed and made known. Most of the audio and visual materials are dependent on the written word.

Writing, however, is often the source of great pain and anxiety. It is remarkable how hard it is for students to sit down quietly and trust their own creativity. There seems to be a deep-seated resistance to writing. I have experienced this resistance myself over and over again. Even after many years of writing, I experience real fear when I face the empty page. Why am I so afraid? Sometimes I have an imaginary reader in mind who is looking over my shoulder and rejecting every word I write down. Sometimes I am overwhelmed by the countless books and articles that already have been written and I cannot imagine that I have anything to say that hasn't already been said better by someone else. Sometimes it seems that every sentence fails to express what I really want to say and that written words simply cannot hold what goes on in my mind and heart. So there are many fears and not seldom they paralyze me and make me delay or even abandon my writing plans.

And still, every time I overcome these fears and trust not only my own unique way of being in the world, but also my ability to give words to it, I experience a deep spiritual satisfaction. I have been trying to understand the nature of this satisfaction. What I am gradually discovering is that in the writing I come in touch with the Spirit of God within me and experience how I am led to new places.

Most students of theology think that writing means writing down ideas, insights, or visions. They feel that they first must have something to say before they can put it on paper. For them, writing is little more than recording a pre-existent thought. But with this approach, true writing is impossible. Writing is a process in which we discover what lives in us. The writing itself reveals to us what is alive in us. The deepest satisfaction of writing is precisely that it opens up new spaces within us of which we were not aware before we started to write. To write is to embark on a journey whose final destination we do not know. Thus, writing requires a real act of trust. We have to say to ourselves: "I do not yet know what I carry in my heart, but I trust that it will emerge as I write." Writing is like giving away the few loaves and fishes one has, trusting that they will multiply in the giving. Once we dare to "give away" on paper the few thoughts that come to us, we start discovering how much is hidden underneath these thoughts and gradually come in touch with our own riches.

"Reflections on Theological Education" (unpublished)

LETTER WRITING

OCTOBER 11, 1985

As I was writing letters today, I realized that writing letters is a much more intimate way of communicating than making phone calls. It may sound strange, but I often feel closer to friends I write to than to friends I speak with by phone.

When I write I think deeply about my friends, I pray for them, I tell them my emotions and feelings. I reflect on our relationship and I dwell with them in a very personal way. Over the past few months I have come to enjoy letter writing more and more. In the beginning it seemed like a heavy burden, but now it is a relaxing time of the day. It feels like interrupting work for a conversation with a friend.

The beauty of letter writing is that it deepens friendships and makes them more real. I have also discovered that letter writing makes me pray more concretely for my friends. Early in the morning I spend a little time praying for each person to whom I have written and promised my prayers.

Today I feel surrounded by the friends I am writing to and praying for. Our love for each other is very concrete and life-giving. Thank God for letters, for those who send them and for those who receive them.

The Road to Daybreak

THE STORY OF
THE HYPERVIGILANT NUN

LIMA, PERU, JANUARY 27, 1982

Anyone who has lived awhile in one of the poor sections of Lima tends to warn visiting friends against robbers and pickpockets. "Do not wear your watch visibly on the bus, someone will rip it off;" "Be sure to have a second pair of glasses, someone might pull your glasses from your head to sell the frame;" "Do not let your purse hang loosely from your shoulder, someone might cut the strap and run away with all your money and your papers;" and so on. Such warnings can be heard every day, often coupled with dramatic stories to show that the warnings are necessary.

Today, however, I heard a story about the consequences, not of carelessness but of hypervigilance. A nun who had lived in Lima for quite some time had a friend visiting her. One afternoon, when this friend wanted to go shopping in the market, her experienced host said: "Now, be careful on the buses and in the marketplace. Before you know it, they will grab your money, your purse, and your watch. Be sure to take your watch off and put it in your purse and hold your purse tight under your arm."

Thus warned, the sister went on her way. The bus was crowded as always, and she had to push her way into it, always conscious of the potential robbers around her. While the bus was moving, and the sister was holding on to the handle to keep her balance, she suddenly noticed her watch on the bare arm of a young man leaning against her.

Overcome by the awareness that after all the warnings she had not been able to avoid being robbed, and furious at the shameless thief, she screamed: "You stole my watch, give it back immediately." While saying this, she pulled out her pen and pushed it right into the man's cheek. The reaction was quick. The man, frightened by the aggressive nun and realizing (without understanding her English) that she meant business, quickly took off the watch and gave it to her.

Meanwhile, the bus had come to a stop and this gave the sister the opportunity to get off immediately. She had become so nervous that her only desire was to get home. When she returned to her friend's house with her watch still tightly grasped in her hand, her friend said: "But how, in heaven's name, did this man ever get into your purse?" "I don't know," was the puzzled answer.

Then the sister opened her purse and found her watch tucked safely between her notebooks and papers. In total consternation, she cried out: "My God, now I have two watches—and one of them I stole!" Her hypervigilance had turned her into a robber.

Sometimes we may be more frightened of people than we need to be. Maybe on her next trip to the market, the sister should wear a watch on each arm so that at least one will be stolen.

Gracias! A Latin American Journal

Celebrating
Children

FREIBURG, FEBRUARY 2, 1986

As I return from Hanover to Freiburg I feel grateful, especially for the ability to be with friends and to play with their children.

I enjoyed seeing little Eric discover his world. He is in the "one-word" stage. No sentences yet. Just words. Papa, Mami, *wasser, brot, heiss, kalt* . . . He is giving names to his world. He is fulfilling the great call which God gave to human beings: naming. "From the soil Yahweh God fashioned all the wild animals and all the birds of heaven. These he brought to the man to see what he would call them; each one was to bear the name the man would give it. The man gave names to all the cattle, all the birds of heaven and all the wild animals" (Gen. 2:19–20).

Giving names is one of the most human of tasks. I saw Eric's joy and excitement when he pronounced a new word. The world is losing its strangeness for him. It is gradually becoming a familiar place. It is becoming his world, where he can feel at home.

I am still doing what Eric does: attaching words to unfamiliar realities—emotions, feelings, passions, visions, dreams, pains, joys, fears, and hopes. I feel his excitement when I find words for an experience which I couldn't name for a long time. I cry out in joy: "Now I can say it! It is painful, but I have a word for it now and I can share it with others." I am spending a major part of my life trying to name the world. It is a task God has given to all of us, a task which never ends. Eric and I are true brothers. We both try to find the right words and are excited if we find them.

Meanwhile, three-month-old Falk-Henry is still so helpless. Mostly he looks very happy and content, but when he cries, he cannot yet say what his problem is. We often feel helpless too. But within fifteen months Falk will also give words to the world, he will be less helpless and an even greater joy to those around him.

Unpublished journal

LIMA, PERU, JANUARY 28, 1982

If anything has affected me deeply since I have been living in Pamplona Alta, it has been the children. I have realized that since my eighteenth year I have not been around children. The seminary, the university, and all the teaching positions that followed were the worlds of young adults, worlds in which children and old people hardly entered. Yet here I am surrounded by boys and girls running up to me, giving me kisses, climbing up to my shoulders, throwing balls at me, and constantly asking for some sign of interest in their lives.

The children always challenge me to live in the present. They want me to be with them here and now, and they find it hard to understand that I might have other things to do or to think about. After all my experiences with psychotherapy, I suddenly have discovered the great healing power of children. Every time Pablito, Johnny, and Maria run up to welcome me, pick up my suitcase, and bring me to my "roof-room," I marvel at their ability to be fully present to me. Their uninhibited expression of affection and their willingness to receive it pull me directly into the moment and invite me to celebrate life where it is found. Whereas in the past coming home meant time to study, to write letters, and to prepare for classes, it now first of all means time to play.

In the beginning I had to get used to finding a little boy under my bed, a little girl in my closet, and a teenager under my table, but now I am disappointed when I find my friends asleep at night. I did not know what to expect when I came to Pamplona Alta. I wondered how the poverty and the lack of good food and good housing would affect me; I was afraid of becoming depressed by the misery I would see. But God showed me something else first: affectionate, open, and playful children who are telling me about love and life in ways no book was ever able to do. I now realize that only when I can enter with the children into their joy will I be able to enter also with them into their poverty and pain. God obviously wants me to walk into the world of suffering with a little child on each hand.

Gracias! A Latin American Journal

Celebrating
Life

When we speak about celebration we tend rather easily to bring
to mind happy, pleasant, gay festivities in which we can forget
for a while the hardships of life and immerse ourselves in an
atmosphere of music, dance, drinks, laughter, and a lot of cozy
small-talk. But celebration in the Christian sense has very little
to do with this. Celebration is possible only through the deep
realization that life and death are never found completely separate. Celebration can really come about only where fear and
love, joy and sorrow, tears and smiles can exist together.
Celebration is the acceptance of life in a constantly increasing
awareness of its preciousness. And life is precious not only
because it can be seen, touched, and tasted, but also because it
will be gone one day.

When we celebrate a wedding we celebrate a union as well as
a departure; when we celebrate death we celebrate lost friendship as well as gained liberty. There can be tears after weddings
and smiles after funerals. We can indeed make our sorrows, just
as much as our joys, a part of our celebration of life in the deep
realization that life and death are not opponents but do, in fact,
kiss each other at every moment of our existence.

When we are born we become free to breathe on our own
but lose the safety of our mother's body; when we go to school
we are free to join a greater society but lose a particular place in
our family; when we marry we find a new partner but lose the

special tie we had with our parents; when we find work we win our independence by making our own money but lose the stimulation of teachers and fellow students; when we receive children we discover a new world but lose much of our freedom to move; when we are promoted we become more important in the eyes of others but lose the chance to take many risks; when we retire we finally have the chance to do what we want but lose the support of being wanted.

When we have been able to celebrate life in all these decisive moments where gaining and losing—that is, life and death—touched each other all the time, we will be able to celebrate even our own dying because we have learned from life that those who lose it can find it (cf. Matt. 16:25).

Creative Ministry

A Prayer to the God of Ebb and Flow

Dear Lord, today I thought of the words of Vincent van Gogh: "It is true there is an ebb and flow, but the sea remains the sea." You are the sea. Although I experience many ups and downs in my emotions and often feel great shifts and changes in my inner life, you remain the same. Your sameness is not the sameness of a rock, but the sameness of a faithful lover. Out of your love I came to life; by your love I am sustained; and to your love I am always called back. There are days of sadness and days of joy; there are feelings of guilt and feelings of gratitude; there are moments of failure and moments of success; but all of them are embraced by your unwavering love.

My only real temptation is to doubt in your love, to think of myself as beyond the reach of your love, to remove myself from the healing radiance of your love. To do these things is to move into the darkness of despair.

O Lord, sea of love and goodness, let me not fear too much the storms and winds of my daily life, and let me know that there is ebb and flow but that the sea remains the sea. Amen.

A Cry for Mercy

NOTES:

[1]Thomas Merton, *The Way of Chuang Tzu*, New York: New Directions, 1965, p. 154.

II

SPRINGS OF HOPE:
HOLINESS AND
HUMANNESS

I pray that this will be my ministry:
to join people on their journey and
to open their eyes to see you.

A Cry for Mercy

Who Is the Lord to Whom I Pray?

GENESEE ABBEY, AUGUST 12, 1974

Speaking about prayer, I asked [Abbot] John Eudes a question that seemed very basic and a little naive: "When I pray, to whom do I pray?" "When I say 'Lord,' what do I mean?"

John Eudes responded very differently than I expected. He said, "This is the real question, this is the most important question you can raise; at least this is the question that you can make your most important question."

He stressed with great and convincing emphasis that if I really wanted to take that question seriously, I should realize that there would be little room left for other things. "Except," he said, smiling, "when the question exhausts you so much that you need to read *Newsweek* for a little relaxation!

"It is far from easy," John Eudes said, "to make that question the center of your meditation. You will discover that it involves every part of yourself because the question Who is the Lord to whom I pray? leads directly to the question Who am I who wants to pray to the Lord? And then you will soon wonder Why is the Lord of justice also the Lord of love; the God of fear also the God of gentle compassion? This leads you to the center of meditation. Is there an answer? Yes and no. You will find out in your meditation. You might someday have a flash of understanding even while the question still remains and pulls you closer to God. But it is not a question that can be simply one of your questions. In a way, it needs to be your only question around which all that you do finds its place. It requires a certain decision to make that question the center of your meditation. If you do so, you will realize that you are embarking on a long road, a very long road."

Genesee Diary

From Magic to Faith

During the first five years of life we have to take three big steps out of the magical world in which we are born.

1

During the first eighteen months we come to the somewhat frustrating discovery that we are not the center of the world.

Most will agree that there are people and things outside of us which will continue to exist even when we don't. This is, however, not so self-evident as it seems. It is only through a long and often frustrating experience that we are able to discover the objective world. As a baby in the mother's womb, everything is there for us; mother is a part of ourself. Later, it can be quite a painful experience to discover that our cry does not create the milk, that our smile does not produce the mother, that our needs do not evoke their own satisfaction. Only gradually do we discover our mother as the Other, as not just a part of ourself. Every time we experience that we are not ruling the world by our feelings, thoughts, and actions, we are forced to realize that there are other persons, things, and events which have their autonomy.

Therefore, the first step out of the magical world is the

discovery of an objective reality. It can happen that we reach this objectivity only partially. Although we slowly unfold and become able to stand on our own feet and point to the things around us as objective realities available for our curious mind, this may not happen so easily in the religious dimension.

Many mature, successful people in this life often might still treat God as part of themselves. God is the factotum which comes in handy in times of illness, shock, final exams, in every situation in which we feel insecure. And if it does not work, the only reaction may be to cry louder. Far from becoming the Other, whose existence does not depend on mine, God might remain the easy frame which fits best around the edges of my security. Great anxiety, caused by internal or external storms, can sometimes force us to regress to this level of religion. This regression may even save our life. It gives us something to hold on to, a medal or a candle which can keep us together. It may be a very helpful form of religion; but certainly it is not a mature form of religion.

Intimacy

2

The second step out of our magical world is the formation of language. Somewhere between our eighteenth month of life and our third birthday we started mumbling our first sounds which slowly developed into words, sentences, and a language. Although it may be disappointing that there are things around us which do not belong to us, by words we can take revenge, because our first words give us a mysterious power over things. Like an American who is excited to discover that his first French word, *garçon*, really brings the waiter to his table, the child experiences not so much the mastery of words but mastery of objects. It takes quite a while before we can detach the word from the object and give it a symbolic function. . . .

Is there not something of this magical world left in us if we feel that we will be saved if we say our prayers every day, or if we at least keep the custom of the three Hail Marys before going to bed? It seems difficult to overcome this word-magic. . . . We seem to be saying, "God cannot do anything to us now. We did what God asked us to do, and now it is God's turn to pay us back." Our prayers give us some power over God instead of engaging us in a real dialogue.

Intimacy

3

The third step out of the magical world is the formation of our conscience. . . .

Conscience becomes possible by the process of identification. We develop the capacity to interiorize certain aspects of the personality of another person, to make them a part of ourselves. In the case of moral development, we take over judgments, standards, and values of beloved persons and incorporate them into our own personality. . . .

When Sigmund Freud wrote his *Future of an Illusion*, he irritated and deeply disturbed the faithful by saying that religion is the continuation of infantile life and that God is the projection of the ever-present desire for shelter.

Freud's task was to cure people, that is, to make them become more mature. And looking at the many people in his office in Vienna who suffered from their religion more than they were saved by it, he tried to unmask their projections. The psychiatrist Rumke summarizes Freud's position when he writes:

When man matures completely he realizes that his God image, often a father-God image, is a reincarnation of the infantile worldly father, loved and feared. God is apparently no more than a projection. If that which blocks his growth is taken away, the image fades. Man distinguishes good from evil according to his own standards. He has conquered the remainder of his neurosis, which was all that his religion was.[1]

What is important in this context is that Freud was not altogether wrong. We often stay in this magical and infantile world in which God is as nice to have around as the comforting blanket of Linus in "Peanuts." For many, religion is really not very much more than Freud found it to be, and for all of us, so many of our religious experiences are clothed in images of childhood that it is often very difficult to say where our infantilism ends and our religion begins.

Intimacy

MATURE RELIGION

A mature religion is integral in nature—that means that it is flexible enough to integrate all new knowledge within its frame of reference and keep pace with all the new discoveries of the human mind. It indeed takes the cross into the spacecraft. Going to school means starting on the road to science, and if religion does not follow the same road with an open and critical eye, the grown adult who flies the ocean in superjets might be religiously still content with a tricycle. Essential for mature religion is the constant willingness to shift gears, to integrate new insights, and to revise our positions.

Intimacy

The Search for God

LIVING THE QUESTIONS

Teachers can only be teachers when there are students who want to be students. Without a question, an answer is experienced as manipulation; without a struggle, help is considered interference; and without the desire to learn, the offer to teach is easily felt as oppression. Therefore, our first task is not to offer information, advice, or even guidance, but to allow others to come into touch with their own struggles, pains, doubts, and insecurities—in short, to affirm their life as quest.

That is quite a difficult task since it runs counter to the mainstream of education that wants to give knowledge to understand, skills to control, and power to conquer. In religious education, we encounter a God who cannot be understood, we discover realities that cannot be controlled, and we realize that our hope is hidden not in the possession of power but in the confession of weakness. As long as a religion is perceived by the student and treated by the teacher as another field to be mastered—with competition, grades, and rewards—only hostility and resentment can be expected. The main questions of religion—Who am I? Where have I come from? Where am I going?—are not questions with an answer but questions that open us to new questions which lead us deeper into the unspeakable mystery of existence.

What needs affirmation is the validity of these questions. What needs to be said is: "Yes, yes indeed, these are the questions. Don't hesitate to raise them. Don't be afraid to enter them." Teaching religion, therefore, is first of all the affirmation of the basic human quest for meaning. Teaching means the creation of the space in which the validity of the questions does not depend on the availability of answers but on their capacity to open us to new perspectives and horizons. Teaching means to allow all the daily experiences of life such as loneliness, fear, anxiety, insecurity, doubt, ignorance, need for affection, support, and understanding, and the long cry for love to be recognized as an essential part of the quest for meaning.

This quest, precisely because it does not lead to ready answers but to new questions, is extremely painful and at times even excruciating. But when we ignore, and thus deny, this pain in our students, we deprive them of their humanity. The pain of the human search is a growing pain. When we prevent that pain from entering into consciousness, we suffocate the forces of human development. In our technocratic and commercial world, where the constant suggestion is made that for all human pains—loneliness and death included—there is a booklet, a pill, or an insurance company, the whole of existence easily becomes plastic. Then death begins to show itself in boredom, undirected aggression, or self-destructive violence.

When we put a heavy taboo on the great questions of life, we become servants of death.

If there is any book in the Bible which shows the harm done by denying the human search, it is the book of Job. In the midst of his misery, Job cries out: "God damn the day I was born and the night I was thrust from the womb . . . why couldn't I have died as they pulled me out of the womb? Why were there arms to hold me and breasts to keep me alive? If only I had strangled or drowned on my way to the light!"

And what did his friends—Eliphaz, Bildad, and Zophar— say? They could not endure his questions and shouted at him:

"How long will you go on talking, filling our ears with trash?"
And bypassing his cry, they started to defend God and themselves. But Job said: "I am sick of your consolations. How long
will you fling these words at me? . . . I, too, could say such
things if you were in my place. I could bury you with accusa-
tions and sneer at you in my piety." Job received no help from
his friends. By denying his painful questions, they in fact drove
him into deeper despair.

Thus, to be a teacher means, first of all, not to deny but to
affirm the search, to allow the painful questions to be raised.
This means that we must constantly avoid the temptation to be
easy defenders of God, the church, the tradition, or whatever
we feel called to defend. Experience suggests that such glib
apologetics animate in students only hostility and anger, and
finally a growing alienation from whom or what we are trying
to defend. All teachers of religion are constantly in danger of
becoming like Job's friends, anxiously avoiding the painful search
and nervously filling the gap created by unanswerable questions.

"Living The Questions: The
Spirituality of the Religion Teacher"
Union Seminary Quarterly Review, Fall 1976

LIMITS OF
OUR HUMAN SYMBOLS

Last year I met a Methodist minister from South Africa who
came to the United States for an extra year of training. He said:

> When I felt called to become a minister, the Methodist
> Church sent me immediately to a parish where I preached
> and taught religion with much conviction and great success. I
> felt I knew who God was and what people had to do to be
> saved. But then after three years the Church sent me to the
> seminary.

I asked him what he learned there. "Nothing really," he said.

I started to question myself, to doubt and to wonder how I could have been so sure about so many things. I read many commentaries on the Bible. I studied Barth, Bultmann, Rahner, and Schillebeeckx. I heard about Kierkegaard, Sartre, Heidegger, and Camus and I finally realized that I really didn't know who God or man was. But that growing ignorance made me gentle and understanding, and when I returned to the parish I at least could hear and listen to the painful search of my own parishioners.

The seminary education had emptied him out and made him receptive to the quest for meaning in many people's lives. Instead of clinging to his own small preconceptions, he slowly discovered that God was not just father or brother, love or justice, awesome or gentle, but that God becomes known to us by our constant confession of the limits of our human symbols.

Theological formation is the gradual and often painful discovery of God's incomprehensibility. You can be competent in many things, but you cannot be competent in God.

"From Resentment to Gratitude"

GOD EXISTS

BOLIVIA, NOVEMBER 21, 1981

God exists. When I can say this with all that I am, I have the "gnosis" (the knowledge of God) about which St. John speaks and the "Memoria Dei" (the memory of God) about which St. Basil writes. To say with all that we have, think, feel, and are "God exists" is the most world-shattering statement that a human being can make. When we make that statement, all the distinctions between intellectual, emotional, affective, and spiritual understanding fall away and there is only one truth left to acclaim: God exists. When we say this from the heart, everything trembles in heaven and on earth. Because when God exists, all that *is* flows from God.

When I want to know if I ever have come to the true knowledge, the *gnosis*, of God's existence, I have simply to allow myself to become aware of how I experience myself. It doesn't take much to realize that I am constantly with myself. I am aware of all of the various parts of my body, and I "know" when I am hurting and when not. I am aware of my desire for food and clothing and shelter. I am aware of my sexual urges and my need for intimacy and community. I am aware of my feelings of pity, compassion, and solidarity, my ability to be of service and my hope to give a helping hand. I am aware of my intellectual, physical, and artistic skills and my drive to use them. I am aware of my anger, my lust, my feelings of revenge and resentment, and even at times of my desire to harm. Indeed, what is central to me is: *I exist*. My own existence fills me, and wherever I turn I find myself again locked in my own self-awareness: I exist. Although experiences of hatred are different from experiences of love, and although a desire for power is different from a desire to serve, they all are the same insofar as they identify *my* existence as what *really* counts.

However, as soon as I say "God exists," my existence no longer can remain in the center, because the essence of the knowledge of God reveals my own existence as deriving its total being from God's. That is the true conversion experience. I no longer let the knowledge of my existence be the center from which I derive, project, deduct, or intuit the existence of God; I suddenly or slowly find my own existence revealed to me in and through the knowledge of God. Then it becomes real for me that I can love myself and my neighbor only because God has loved me first.

The life-converting experience is not the discovery that I have choices to make that determine the way I live out my existence but the answer that my existence itself is not in the center.

Once I "know" God, that is, once I experience God's love as the love in which all my human experiences are anchored, I can only desire one thing: to be in that love. "Being" anywhere else, then, is shown to be illusory and eventually lethal.

Gracias! A Latin American Journal

Preaching and
Ministry

In 1857 Anthony Trollope wrote in *Barchester Towers*: "There is, perhaps, no greater hardship at present inflicted on mankind in civilized and free countries than the necessity of listening to sermons" (cf., *U.S. Catholic*, July 1970, "Let's Abolish the Sunday Sermon," by Daphne D. C. Pochin Mould). I would not be surprised to find many people today who are willing to agree with him.

Creative Ministry

THE PROBLEM
OF THE MESSAGE

If we say that preaching means announcing the good news, it is important to realize that for most people there is absolutely no news in the sermon. Practically nobody listens to a sermon with the expectation of hearing something they did not already know. They have heard about Jesus—His disciples, His sayings, His miracles, His death and resurrection—at home, in kindergarten, in grade school, in high school, and in college so often and in so many different ways and forms that the last thing they expect to come from a pulpit is any news.

And the core of the Gospel—"You must love the Lord your

God with all your heart, with all your soul, and with all your mind and you must love your neighbor as yourself"—has been repeated so often and so persistently that it has lost, for the majority of people, even the slightest possibility of evoking any response. They have heard it from the time of their earliest childhood and will continue to hear it until they are dead—unless, of course, they become so bored on the way that they refuse to place themselves any longer in a situation in which they will be exposed to this redundant information.

It is fascinating to see how people sit up straight, eyes wide open, when the preacher starts his sermon with a little secular story by way of appetizer but immediately turn on their sleeping signs and curl up in a more comfortable position when the famous line comes: "And this, my brothers and sisters, is exactly what Jesus meant when He said . . ." From then on most preachers are alone, relying only on the volume of their voices or the idiosyncrasies of their movements to keep in contact.

It is indeed sad to say that the name of Jesus for many people has lost most of its mobilizing power. Too often the situation is like the one in the Catholic school where the teacher asked: "Children, who invented the steam engine?" Everyone was silent until finally a little boy sitting in the back of the class raised his finger and said in a dull voice and with watery eyes: "I guess it is Jesus again."

When a message has become so redundant that it has completely lost the ability to evoke any kind of creative response, it can hardly be considered a message any longer. And if you feel you cannot avoid being present physically at its presentation, you at least can close your eyes and mind and drop out.

Creative Ministry

THE PROBLEM
OF THE MESSENGER

1

If there is any posture that disturbs a suffering man or woman, it is aloofness. The tragedy of Christian ministry is that many who are in great need, many who seek an attentive ear, a word of support, a forgiving embrace, a firm hand, a tender smile, or even a stuttering confession of inability to do more, often find their ministers distant people who do not want to burn their fingers. They are unable or unwilling to express their feelings of affection, anger, hostility, or sympathy. The paradox indeed is that those who want to be for "everyone" find themselves often unable to be close to anyone. When everybody becomes my "neighbor," it is worth wondering whether anybody can really become my "proximus," that is, the one who is most close to me.

. . . No one can help anyone without becoming involved, without entering with his or her whole person into the painful situation, without taking the risk of becoming hurt, wounded, or even destroyed in the process. . . .

Who can save a child from a burning house without taking the risk of being hurt by the flames? Who can listen to a story of loneliness and despair without taking the risk of experiencing similar pains and even losing precious peace of mind? In short, "Who can take away suffering without entering it?"

The great illusion of leadership is to think that others can be led out of the desert by someone who has never been there.

The Wounded Healer

It is sad that most ministers have more hours of training in how to talk and be with people than how to talk and be with God.

The Living Reminder

2

One of the greatest ironies of the history of Christianity is that its leaders constantly gave in to the temptation of power—political power, military power, economic power, or moral and spiritual power—even though they continued to speak in the name of Jesus, who didn't cling to his divine power, but emptied himself and became as we are. The temptation to consider power a useful instrument in the proclamation of the Gospel is the greatest of all. We keep hearing from others, as well as saying to ourselves, that having power, provided it is used in the service of God and your fellow human beings, is a good thing. With this rationalization, crusades took place, inquisitions were organized, Indians were enslaved, positions of great influence were desired, episcopal palaces, splendid cathedrals, and opulent seminaries were built, and much moral manipulation of conscience was engaged in. Every time we see a major crisis in the history of the Church, such as the great schism of the tenth century, the reformation of the sixteenth century, or the immense secularization of the twentieth century, we always see that a major cause of rupture is the power exercised by those who claim to be followers of the poor and powerless Jesus.

What makes the temptation of power so seemingly irresistible? Maybe it is that power offers an easy substitute for the hard task of love. It seems easier to be God than to love God, easier to control people than to love people, easier to own life than to love life. Jesus asks, "Do you love me?" We ask, "Can we sit at your right hand and your left hand in your Kingdom?" (see Matt. 20:21) Ever since the snake said, "The day you eat of this tree your eyes will be open and you will be like gods, knowing good from evil" (Gen. 3:5), we have been tempted to replace love by power. Jesus lived that temptation in the most agonizing way from the desert to the Cross, and the long painful history of the Church is the history of people who chose power over love, control over the cross, being a leader over being led.

One thing is clear to me, that the temptation of power is greatest when intimacy is a threat. Much Christian leadership is exercised by people who do not know how to develop a healthy intimate relationship and have chosen for power and control instead. Many Christian empire builders have been people unable to give and receive love.

"With Outstretched Hands" lecture given at Center for Human Development, Washington, D.C., September 21, 1987

THE PROBLEM
OF THE UNCONVERTED

Learning is meant to lead to a redemptive insight into the human condition. But do we always desire insight? Bernard Lonergan writes:

> Just as insight can be desired, so, too, it can be unwanted. Beside the love of light, there can be a love of darkness. If prepossessions and prejudices notoriously vitiate theoretical investigations, much more easily can elementary passions bias understanding in practical and personal matters. To exclude an insight is also to exclude the further questions that would arise from it and the complementary insights that would carry it towards a rounded and balanced viewpoint. To lack that fuller view results in behavior that generates misunderstanding both in ourselves and in others. To suffer such incomprehension favours a withdrawal from the outer drama of human living into the inner drama of phantasy. [2]

Lonergan calls such an aberration of understanding a "scotosis," derived from the Greek word *skotos*, which means "darkness," and the resultant blind spot a "scotoma." By introducing these terms, he has helped us to come to a better understanding of the massive resistance against learning. For it is exactly this scotosis that prevents us from really dealing with those factors that are crucial today in our human struggle. By this scotosis, this exclusion of painful insights, we prevent our own experience from becoming part of the learning process and become like unengaged spectators in the procession of life.

I am trying to say very simple and obvious things here. But if it is true that the most obvious things can easily become the most threatening things to us, then perhaps they also can become the easiest subjects of scotosis.

Scotosis means long and fierce discussions about justice and equality while we hate our teacher or ignore the needs of our fellow students. Scotosis means endless academic quarrels in a world filled with atrocities and much talk about hunger by people suffering from overweight. Scotosis allows church people to indulge in comfortable discussions about the Kingdom of God while they should know that God is with the poor, the sick, the hungry, and the dying. In Lonergan's words: "Scotosis means an aberration which prevents the emergence into consciousness of perspectives that would give rise to unwanted insights" (op. cit., p. 192). It is indeed startling to discover how we keep ourselves free from those unwanted insights.

Creative Ministry

THE AUTHENTIC MESSENGER

Preachers who want to be real leaders are those who are able to put the full range of their life-experiences—their experiences in prayer, in conversation, and in their lonely hours—at the disposal of those who ask them. Pastoral care does not mean running around nervously trying to redeem people, to save them at the last moment, or to put them on the right track by a good idea, an intelligent remark, or practical advice. Pastoral care means: offering your own life-experience to your fellow travelers and, as Paul Simon sings, to lay yourself down like a bridge over troubled water.

Creative Ministry

When we listen to preachers who are really available to themselves and, therefore, able to offer their own life experience as a source of recognition, we no longer have to be afraid to face our own condition and that of our world because the one who stands in front of us is the living witness that insight makes us free and does not create new anxieties. Only then can indifference and irritation be removed, only then can the Word of God, which has been repeated so often but understood so little, find fertile ground and be rooted in the human heart.

Creative Ministry

Every time real preaching occurs, the Crucifixion is realized again: for preachers cannot bring others to the light without having entered the darkness of the Cross themselves. Perhaps Anthony Trollope was right when he said that the necessity of listening to sermons is the greatest hardship inflicted on humanity in civilized and free countries. But if we want our countries to become really free and civilized, let us hope that there always will be men and women to accept the difficult challenge of preaching and lead their people through their own darkness to the Light of God.

Creative Ministry

THE PERFECT MESSENGER

A Story from the Desert Fathers:
Three Fathers used to go and visit blessed Anthony every year, and two of them used to discuss their thoughts and the salvation of their souls with him, but the third always remained silent and did not ask him anything. After a long time, Abba Anthony said to him: "You often come here to see me, but you never ask me anything," and the other replied, "It is enough to see you, Father."[3]

The Way of the Heart

A Preacher's Prayer

Dear Lord, you have sent me into this world to preach your word. So often the problems of the world seem so complex and intricate that your word strikes me as embarrassingly simple. Many times I feel tongue-tied in the company of people who are dealing with the world's social and economic problems.

But you, O Lord, said, "Be clever as serpents and innocent as doves." Let me retain innocence and simplicity in the midst of this complex world. I realize that I have to be informed, that I have to study the many aspects of the problems facing the world, and that I have to try to understand as well as possible the dynamics of our contemporary society. But what really counts is that all this information, knowledge, and insight allow me to speak more clearly and unambiguously your truthful word. Do not allow evil powers to seduce me with the complexities of the world's problems, but give me the strength to think clearly, speak freely, and act boldly in your service. Give me the courage to show the dove in a world so full of serpents. Amen.

A Cry for Mercy

Holiness, Humanness, and Prayer

TV AND PRAYER

I am reading a fascinating chapter from Jerry Mander's book *Four Arguments for the Elimination of Television*. The main idea is: "We evolve into the images we carry in our minds. We become what we see. And in today's America, what most of us see is one hell of a lot of television."

I had heard stories about Vietnam veterans who, during their first real battle, thought that it was just another war movie and were shocked when those they killed did not stand up and walk away. I had read that Vincent van Gogh saw the real world as an imitation of the paintings he saw in the museum. I had noticed how children often are more excited about the repeated advertisements on television than about the movie they interrupt. But I had never fully thought through the enormous impact of the artificially imposed images on my thoughts, feelings, and actions. When it is true that the image you carry in your mind can affect your physical, mental, and emotional life, then it becomes a crucial question as to which images we expose ourselves or allow ourselves to be exposed.

All of this is important to me because it has profound spiritual implications. Prayer also has much to do with imagining.

When I bring myself into the presence of God, I imagine God in many ways: as a loving father, a supporting sister, a caring mother, a severe teacher, an honest judge, a fellow traveler, an intimate friend, a gentle healer, a challenging leader, a demanding taskmaster. All these "personalities" create images in my mind that affect not only what I think but also how I actually experience myself. I believe that true prayer makes us into what we imagine. To pray to God leads to becoming like God.

When St. Ignatius proposes that we use all our senses in our meditation, he does more than offer a technique to help us concentrate on the mysteries of God's revelation. He wants us to imagine the reality of the divine as fully as possible so that we can slowly be divinized by that reality. Divinization is, indeed, the goal of all prayer and meditation. This divinization allows St. Paul to say: "I live now not with my own life but with the life of Christ who lives in me" (Gal. 2:20).

The more we come to depend on the images offered to us by those who try to distract us, entertain us, use us for their purposes, and make us conform to the demands of a consumer society, the easier it is for us to lose our identity. These imposed images actually make us into the world which they represent, a world of hatred, violence, lust, greed, manipulation, and oppression. But when we believe that we are created in the image of God and come to realize that Christ came to let us reimagine this, then meditation and prayer can lead us to our true identity.

Gracias! A Latin American Journal

GRACE AT MEALS

I have come to realize how hard it is to have a real spiritual conversation. I keep wondering how people with deep religious convictions can speak together at table about the life of the

Spirit. What did Jesus speak about at table? It seems that for Jesus the meal was the place and time to preach the good news. For me that is a real challenge. It always strikes me how grateful people are for a good spiritual conversation, but also how hard it is to make such a conversation happen. Most conversations are chains of free association in which people simply drift from one subject to another, often guided by little else than what happens to come into their minds.

When an enormous spiritual hunger grows among people, churches may not always be the best places to offer "solid food." Meals with friends who have developed the art of spiritual communication might be much better places. Yet it often seems that we have lost this art.

Unpublished journal

WE MODERN WESTERNERS

We modern Westerners are so busy with ourselves, so preoccupied with the question of whether we do justice to our own selves, that the experience of the "transcendent" becomes practically impossible. In the way of thinking which involves talking, discussing, analyzing, and criticizing, in which one opinion asks the other for attention, in which belief is replaced more and more by an endless list of conceptions, opinions, visions, and ideas which whirl around as paper boats on the sea—in this way of thinking there is scarcely room for the Spirit who speaks whenever we are silent and who comes in whenever we have emptied ourselves. Instead of making ourselves susceptible to the experience of the transcendent God, we, busy about many things, begin to seek after the small, flighty sensations brought about by artificial stimulation of the senses.

Thomas Merton: A Contemplative Critic

PRAYING
IN A BUSY WORLD

In a society that seems to be filled with urgencies and emergencies, prayer appears to be an unnatural form of behavior. Without fully realizing it, we have accepted the idea that "doing things" is more important than prayer and have come to think of prayer as something for times when there is nothing urgent to do. While we might agree verbally, or even intellectually, with someone who stresses the importance of prayer, we have become children of an impatient world to such an extent that our behavior often expresses the view that prayer is a waste of time.

This predicament shows how necessary it is to view prayer as a discipline. Concentrated human effort is necessary because prayer is not our most natural response to the world. Left to our own impulses, we will always want to do something else before we pray. Often, what we want to do seems so unquestionably good—setting up a religious education program, helping with a soup kitchen, listening to people's problems, visiting the sick, planning the liturgy, working with prisoners or mental patients—that it is hard to realize that even these things can be done with impatience and so become signs of our own needs rather than of God's compassion.

Therefore, prayer is in many ways the criterion of Christian life. Prayer requires that we stand in God's presence with open hands, naked and vulnerable, proclaiming to ourselves and to others that without God we can do nothing. This is difficult in a climate where the predominant counsel is "Do your best and God will do the rest." When life is divided into "our best" and "God's rest," we have turned prayer into a last resort to be used only when all our own resources are depleted. Then even the Lord has become the victim of our impatience. Discipleship does not mean to use God when we can no longer function ourselves. On the contrary, it means to recognize that we can do nothing at all, but that God can do everything through us. As disciples, we find not some but all of our strength, hope, courage, and confidence in God. Therefore, prayer must be our first concern.

Compassion

WHAT DOES IT MEAN TO PRAY?

Praying is no easy matter. It demands a relationship in which you allow the other to enter into the very center of your person, to speak there, to touch the sensitive core of your being, and allow the other to see so much that you would rather leave in darkness. And when do you really want to do that? Perhaps you would let the other come across the threshold to say something, to touch something, but to allow the other into that place where your life gets its form, that is dangerous and calls for defense.

The resistance to praying is like the resistance of tightly clenched fists. This image shows the tension, the desire to cling tightly to yourself, a greediness which betrays fear. The story about an old woman brought to a psychiatric center exemplifies an attitude. She was wild, swinging at everything in sight and scaring everyone so much that the doctors had to take everything away from her. But there was one small coin which she gripped in her fist and would not give up. In fact, it took two men to pry open that squeezed hand. It was as though she would lose her very self along with the coin. If they deprived her of that last possession, she would have nothing more, and be nothing more. That was her fear.

When we are invited to pray we are asked to open our tightly clenched fists and to give up our last coin. But who wants to do that? A first prayer, therefore, is often a painful prayer, because you discover you don't want to let go. You hold fast to what is familiar even if you aren't proud of it. You find yourself saying: "That's just how it is with me. I would like it to be different, but it can't be now. That's just the way it is, and that's the way I'll have to leave it." Once you talk like that you've already given up the belief that your life might be otherwise, you've already let the hope for a new life float by. Since you wouldn't dare to put a question mark behind a bit of your own experience with all its attachments, you have wrapped yourself up in the destiny of facts.

You feel it is safer to cling to a sorry past than to trust in a new future. So you fill your hands with small, clammy coins which you don't want to surrender. . . .

Detachment is often understood as letting loose of what is attractive. But it can also mean being attached to what is repulsive. You can become attached to your own hate. As long as you look for retaliation, you are riveted to your own past. Sometimes it appears as though you would lose yourself along with your revenge and hate—so you stand there with balled-up fists, closed to the other who wants to heal. . . .

When you dare to let go and surrender one of those many fears, your hand relaxes and your palms spread out in a gesture of receiving. You must have patience, of course, before your hands are completely open and their muscles relaxed.

You can never fully achieve such an attitude, for behind each fist another one is hiding, and sometimes the process seems endless. Much has happened in your life to make all these fists. . . . At any hour of the day or night you might clench again for fear.

Someone will tell you, "You have to be able to forgive yourself." But that isn't possible. What is possible is to open your hands without fear so the other can blow your sins away. For perhaps it isn't clammy coins, but just a light dust which a

soft breeze will whirl away, leaving only a grin or a chuckle
behind. Then you feel a bit of new freedom, and praying
becomes a joy, a spontaneous reaction to the world and the
people around you. Praying becomes effortless, inspired, and
lively or peaceful and quiet. Then you recognize the festive and
the modest as moments of prayer. You begin to suspect that to
pray is to live.

With Open Hands

Prayer is the way to both the heart of God and the heart of the
world—precisely because they have been joined through the
suffering of Jesus Christ . . . Praying is letting one's own heart
become the place where the tears of God and the tears of God's
children can merge and become tears of hope.

Love in a Fearful Land

How Can I Pray?—
Three Rules

A careful look at the lives of people for whom prayer was indeed "the only thing needed" (see Luke 10:42) shows that three "rules" are always observed: a contemplative reading of the word of God, a silent listening to the voice of God, and a trusting obedience to a spiritual guide. Without the Bible, without silent time, and without someone to direct us, finding our own way to God is very hard and practically impossible.

Reaching Out

1

READING THE SCRIPTURES

In the first place, we have to pay careful attention to the word of God as it is written in the holy scriptures. St. Augustine was converted when he responded to the words of a child saying: "Take and read, take and read."[4] When he took the Bible and started reading the page on which he opened it, he felt that the words he read were directly spoken to him.

To take the holy scriptures and read them is the first thing we have to do to open ourselves to God's call. Reading the scriptures is not as easy as it seems since in our academic world we tend to make anything and everything we read subject to analysis and discussion. But the word of God should lead us first of all to contemplation and meditation. Instead of taking the words apart, we should bring them together in our innermost being; instead of wondering if we agree or disagree, we should wonder which words are directly spoken to us and connect directly with our most personal story. Instead of thinking about the words as potential subjects for an interesting dialogue or paper, we should be willing to let them penetrate into the most hidden corners of our heart, even to those places where no other word has yet found entrance. Then and only then can the word bear fruit as seed sown in rich soil. Only then can we really "hear and understand" (Matt. 13:23).

Reaching Out

2

QUIET TIME FOR GOD

Secondly, we simply need quiet time in the presence of God. Although we want to make all our time time for God, we will never succeed if we do not reserve a minute, an hour, a morning, a day, a week, a month, or whatever period of time for God and God alone.

This asks for much discipline and risk-taking because we always seem to have something more urgent to do and "just sitting there" and "doing nothing" often disturbs us more than it helps. But there is no way around this. Being useless and silent in the presence of our God belongs to the core of all prayer. In the beginning we often hear our own unruly inner noises more loudly than God's voice. This is at times very hard to tolerate.

But slowly, very slowly, we discover that the silent time makes us quiet and deepens our awareness of ourselves and God. Then, very soon, we start missing these moments when we are deprived of them, and before we are fully aware of it an inner momentum has developed that draws us more and more into silence and closer to that still point where God speaks to us.

Contemplative reading of the holy scriptures and silent time in the presence of God belong closely together. The word of God draws us into silence; silence makes us attentive to God's word. . . .

Reaching Out

3

FINDING A SPIRITUAL GUIDE

But word and silence both need guidance. How do we know that we are not deluding ourselves, that we are not selecting those words that best fit our passions, that we are not just listening to the voice of our own imagination? Many have quoted the scriptures and many have heard voices and seen visions in silence, but only few have found their way to God. Who can judge their own cases? Who can determine if their feelings and insights are leading them in the right direction? Our God is greater than our own heart and mind, and too easily we are tempted to make our heart's desires and our mind's speculations into the will of God.

Therefore, we need a guide, a director, a counselor who helps us to distinguish between the voice of God and all the other voices coming from our own confusion or from dark powers far beyond our control. We need someone who encourages us when we are tempted to give it all up, to forget it all, to just walk away in despair. We need someone who discourages us when we move too rashly in unclear directions or hurry proudly to a nebulous goal. We need someone who can suggest to us when to read and when to be silent, which words to reflect upon and what to do when silence creates much fear and little peace.

Thus, the Bible, silence, and a spiritual director are three important guides in our search for our most personal way to enter into an intimate relationship with God. When we contemplate the scriptures continuously, set some time aside to be silent in the presence of our God, and are willing to submit our experiences with word and silence to a spiritual guide, we can keep ourselves from developing new illusions and open the way to the prayer of our heart.

Reaching Out

TO PRAY IS TO BECOME

GENESEE ABBEY, SEPTEMBER 23, 1974

Often I have said to people, "I will pray for you," but how often did I really enter into the full reality of what that means? When I really bring my friends and the many I pray for into my innermost being and feel their pains, their struggles, their cries in my own soul, then I leave myself, so to speak, and become them, then I have compassion.

Compassion lies at the heart of our prayer for our fellow human beings. When I pray for the world, I become the world;

when I pray for the endless needs of the millions, my soul expands and wants to embrace them all and bring them into the presence of God. But in the midst of that experience I realize that compassion is not mine but God's gift to me. I cannot embrace the world, but God can. I cannot pray, but God can pray in me. When God became as we are, that is, when God allowed all of us to enter into the intimacy of the divine life, it became possible for us to share in God's infinite compassion.

In praying for others, I lose myself and become the other, only to be found by the divine love which holds the whole of humanity in a compassionate embrace.

Genesee Diary

God's Presence and God's Absence

The great mystery of the divine revelation is that God entered into intimacy with us not only by Christ's coming but also by his leaving.

Bonhoeffer writes: "The God who is with us is the God who forsakes us (Mark 15:34). . . . Before God and with God we live without God."[5]

The Living Reminder

God is "beyond," beyond our heart and mind, beyond our feelings and thoughts, beyond our expectations and desires, and beyond all the events and experiences that make up our life. Still God is in the center of all of it. Here we touch the heart of prayer since here it becomes manifest that in prayer the distinction between God's presence and God's absence no longer really distinguishes. In prayer, God's presence is never separated from God's absence and God's absence is never separated from God's presence. God's presence is so much beyond the human experience of being together that it quite easily is perceived as absence. God's absence, on the other hand, is often so deeply felt that it leads to a new sense of God's presence. This is powerfully expressed in Ps. 22:1–5:

My God, my God, why have you deserted me?
How far from saving me, the words I groan!
I call all day, my God, but you never answer,
all night long I call and cannot rest.
Yet, Holy One, you
who make your home in the praises of Israel,
in you our fathers put their trust,
they trusted and you rescued them;
they called to you for help and they were saved,
they never trusted you in vain.

This prayer not only is the expression of the experience of the people of Israel, but also the culmination of the Christian experience. When Jesus spoke these words on the cross, total aloneness and full acceptance touched each other. In that moment of complete emptiness all was fulfilled. In that hour of darkness new light was seen. While death was witnessed, life was affirmed. Where God's absence was most loudly expressed, God's presence was most profoundly revealed.

When God, through the humanity of Jesus, freely chose to share our own most painful experience of divine absence, God became most present to us. It is into this mystery that we enter when we pray.

Reaching Out

GOD'S PRESENCE

GENESEE ABBEY, SEPTEMBER 19, 1974

The experience of God's presence is not void of pain. But the pain is so deep that you do not want to miss it since it is in this pain that the joy of God's presence can be tasted. This seems close to nonsense except in the sense that it is beyond sense and, therefore, hard to capture within the limits of human understanding. The experience of God's unifying presence is an experience in which the distinction between joy and pain seems to be transcended and in which the beginning of a new life is intimated.

Genesee Diary

MINISTRY AND GOD'S PRESENCE

As a seer, the minister reveals a presence that had not been noticed before. The problems of life often overwhelm us. The disappointments and disillusionments in personal and professional life tend to narrow our vision and often blind us to anything beyond our own problems. The concreteness and immediacy of present misery seldom permit sufficient distance to see and experience a larger presence. Ministry is the spiritual act of seeing and helping others see the face of a loving God even where nothing but darkness seems to be present.

This can happen in many ways. A simple, quiet presence can be enough to create a freeing distance that allows someone to discover an unexpected perspective on a seemingly hopeless situation. Sometimes a word spoken with serenity and love can remove blindfolds and open up new horizons. It can be a sermon delivered with conviction, a letter written with care, or a lecture given with clarity. It can also be the simple gesture with water, oil, bread, or wine by which a life can be liberated from the narrowing constraints of momentary stress and new connections made which change the whole landscape of our inner experience. But above all, it can be the concrete act of helping others in their need by which sadness is converted to joy and eyes are opened for a new vision.

"The Monk and The Cripple," *America*, March 15, 1980

MINISTRY AND GOD'S ABSENCE

1

We are living in a culture and social climate which places a great and positive emphasis on presence. We feel that being present is a value as such, and almost always better than being absent. Being present constitutes much of our occupation as ministers: present to patients and students, at services, at Bible groups, at all sorts of charitable meetings, at parties, at dinners, at games—and just present in the streets of our town.

Although this ministry of presence is undoubtedly very meaningful, it always needs to be balanced by a ministry of absence. This is so because it belongs to the essence of a creative ministry constantly to convert the pain of Jesus' absence into a deeper understanding of his presence. But absence can only be converted if it is first of all experienced. Therefore, ministers do not fulfill their whole task when they witness only to the presence of Jesus and do not tolerate the experience of his absence. If it is true that ministers are living memories of Jesus Christ, then they must search for ways in which not only their presence but also their absence reminds people of their Lord. This has some concrete implications. It calls for the art of leaving, for the ability to be articulately absent, and most of all for a creative withdrawal. Let me illustrate.

In our ministry of visitation—hospital visits and home visits— it is essential for patients and parishioners to experience that it is good for them, not only that we come but also that we leave. In this way the memory of our visit can become as important, if not more important, than the visit itself. I am deeply convinced that there is a ministry in which our leaving creates space for God's spirit and in which, by our absence, God can become present in a new way. There is an enormous difference between an absence after a visit and an absence which is the result of not coming at all. Without a coming there can be no leaving, and without a presence absence is only emptiness and not the way to a greater intimacy with God through the spirit.

The words of Jesus, "It is for your good that I leave," should be a part of every pastoral call we make. We have to learn to leave so that the spirit can come. Then we can indeed be remembered as a living witness of God. This shows the importance of being sensitive to the last words we speak before we leave a room or house; it also puts the possibility of a prayer before leaving into a new light. . . .

The Living Reminder

2

The great temptation of the ministry is to celebrate only the presence of Jesus while forgetting his absence. Often the minister is most concerned to make people glad and to create an atmosphere of "I'm okay, you're okay." But in this way everything gets filled up and there is no empty space left for the affirmation of our basic lack of fulfillment. In this way the presence of Jesus is enforced without connection with his absence. Almost inevitably this leads to artificial joy and superficial happiness. It also leads to disillusionment because we forget that it is in memory that Jesus Christ is present. If we deny the pain of his absence we will not be able to taste his sustaining presence either.

The Living Reminder

Ministry is the profession of fools and clowns telling every-one who has ears to hear and eyes to see that life is not a problem to be solved but a mystery to be entered into.

"From Resentment to Gratitude"

THE PRAYER OF PROTEST:
MAY I ARGUE WITH GOD?

GENESEE ABBEY, SEPTEMBER 20, 1974

Abraham Heschel reveals an aspect of spirituality in his discus-sion of the Kotzker that seems practically absent in Christian life and certainly has never been stressed in my life. It is the aspect of protest against God. He writes:

> The refusal to accept the harshness of God's ways in the name of his love was an authentic form of prayer. Indeed, the ancient Prophets of Israel were not in the habit of consenting to God's harsh judgment and did not simply nod, saying, "Thy will be done." They often challenged him, as if to say, "Thy will be changed." They had often countered and even annulled divine decrees.[6] . . . A man who lived by honesty could not be expected to suppress his anxiety when tor-mented by profound perplexity. He had to speak out auda-ciously. Man should never capitulate, even to the Lord.[7]
> . . . There are some forms of suffering that a man must accept with love and bear in silence. There are other agonies to which he must say no.[8]

This attitude shows, in fact, how close the Jew, who can protest against God, feels to God. When I can only relate to God in terms of submission, I am much more distant from God than when I feel free to question divine decrees. Most remark-able, therefore, is that this intimacy with God leads to a feeling that has never been part of my thinking but might be very important: Compassion *for* God.

Heschel tells the beautiful story of the Polish Jew who stopped praying "because of what happened in Auschwitz." Later, however, he started to pray again. When asked, "What made you change your mind?" he answered, "It suddenly dawned upon me to think how lonely God must be; look with whom he is left. I felt sorry for him."[9]

This attitude brings God and God's people very close to each other, because God is known by his people as the one who suffers with them.

Heschel writes: "The cardinal issue, Why does the God of justice and compassion permit evil to persist? is bound up with the problem of how man should aid God so that his justice and compassion prevail."[10] The most powerful sentence of Heschel is: "Faith is the beginning of compassion, of compassion for God. It is when bursting with God's sighs that we are touched by the awareness that *beyond all absurdity* there is meaning, truth, and love."[11] This is an experience of deep mysticism in which active protest and passive surrender are both present, and we struggle with God as Jacob wrestled with the angel.

Genesee Diary

PRAYER AND COMMUNITY

Much that has been said about prayer might create the false impression that prayer is a private, individualistic, and nearly secret affair, so personal and so deeply hidden in our inner life that it can hardly be talked about, even less be shared. The opposite is true. Just because prayer is so personal and arises from the center of our life, it is to be shared with others. Just because prayer is the most precious expression of being human, it needs the constant support and protection of the community to grow and flower. Just because prayer is our highest vocation needing careful attention and faithful perseverance, we cannot allow it to be a private affair. Just because prayer asks for a patient waiting in expectation, it should never become the most individualistic expression of the most individualistic emotion, but should always remain embedded in the life of the community of which we are part. . . .

Reaching Out

Without some form of community, individual prayer cannot be born or developed. Communal and individual prayer belong together as two folded hands. Without community, individual prayer easily degenerates into egocentric and eccentric behavior, but without individual prayer, the prayer of the community quickly becomes a meaningless routine. Individual and community prayer cannot be separated without harm. This explains why spiritual leaders tend to be very critical of those who want to isolate themselves and why they stress the importance of continuing ties with a larger community, where individual prayer can be guided. This also explains why the same leaders have always encouraged the individual members of their communities to spend time and energy in personal prayer, realizing as they do that community alone can never fulfill the desire for the most unique intimate relationship between a human being and his or her God.

Reaching Out

The Spirit of
St. Francis

GENESEE ABBEY, OCTOBER 4, 1974

Chesterton gives a beautiful insight into the conversion of Francis by describing him as the "tumbler for God" who stands on his head for the pleasure of God. By seeing the world upside down "with all the trees and towers hanging head downwards," Francis discovers its dependent nature. The word *dependence* means "hanging." By seeing his world, his city, upside down, Francis saw the same world and the same city but in a different way. "Instead of being merely proud of his strong city because it could not be moved, he would be thankful to God Almighty that it had not been dropped."

This conversion, this turn around, this new view, made it possible for Francis to make praise and thanksgiving his central attitude in a world that he had rediscovered in its most profound dependence on God.

Here, indeed, we reach that mysterious point where asceticism and joy touch each other. Francis, who was a very severe ascetic, is, nevertheless, known as the most joyful of saints. His joy about all that is created was born out of his full realization of its dependence on God. In fasting and poverty, he reminded himself and others of God's lordship. In his songs of praise and thanksgiving, he revealed the beauty of all that is obedient to its Creator.

Genesee Diary

There were many wars, conflicts, and much poverty and misery in the thirteenth century, but we do not remember the political struggles and the socioeconomic events of that century. We remember one man who lived in the midst of it and prayed, prayed, and prayed until his hands and feet were pierced with the wounds of Christ himself. Who will be the St. Francis of our age?

Gracias! A Latin American Journal

In an unpublished manuscript Henri Nouwen wrote in the early seventies:

"When I went to Peru for the first time I was strongly motivated by the burning issues of Latin America. I had heard and read about illiteracy, malnutrition, poor health, infant mortality, and many other problems. I was so overwhelmed by my own privileged position that I could no longer tolerate my 'splendid isolation' and wanted to do something to alleviate the suffering of my fellow human beings of which I had become increasingly aware."

The "something" he eventually did was to resign from his "privileged position" as full professor of pastoral theology with tenure at Yale, and begin preparations for a six-month sojourn in Latin America. His purpose: to seek an answer to the question haunting him over a period of many years: "Does God call me to live and work in Latin America in the years to come?"

Thus in October of 1981 he flew to Peru to touch base with his Maryknoll Missionary hosts, and from there went on to Bolivia for language training. Having completed a three-month course designed to improve his Spanish, he returned to Peru for three months of missionary work "in the field."

The excerpts from his Latin-American journal (Gracias!), which follow, describe a portion of his experience during his three-month stay, from January to March of 1982, living among the poor in the barrios of Lima.

"MY NEW HOUSE"

1

LIMA, PERU, JANUARY 14, 1982

Tonight I finally moved to Pamplona Alta. I have now been in Peru for twelve days, and I have needed all that time to get oriented, meet different Maryknollers, get a feel for the region, and organize my own affairs. It is good to move away from the comfortable American climate of the center house into the Peruvian world.

Pete Ruggere drove me in his blue Volkswagen to my new living quarters with the Oscco-Moreno family. They are his neighbors, and with their help he has built a pleasant room on top of the roof of their house. The word "roof" is a euphemism since this house, like many of the houses in the area, is only half finished. Construction continues at a variable rate depending on money, need, and time. My little room, therefore, might better be seen as the first room built on the second floor.

Since nothing else is finished on the second floor, I have in fact a large terrace looking out over the many houses of the neighborhood. My room consists of four brick walls—painted pink ("the only color I had") by our neighbor Octavio—and a roof made of sheets of metal. There is a door and a window, but the wind and the dust have free access to my home since the builders left a lot of open spaces where walls, window, door, and roof meet. With virtually no rain here and with little cold weather, my small place seems quite comfortable and pleasant.

I often have thought about having a *poustinia*, or small building for prayer on the marketplace, and this new place seems to be just that. It is like a monk's cell between a large sea of houses and people.

I was warmly welcomed by the downstairs family of Sophia and Pablo and their three children, Pablito, Maria, and Johnny. They all showed great kindness to me, and the kids were soon hanging on my arms and legs.

Pete Ruggere, Tom Burns, and Larry Rich live in the next house. There I can go at any time to wash, use the bathroom, eat, listen to music, or watch television. Their house is a section of the house in which Octavio and his wife and eleven children live. The space looks very small to me, and I wonder where and how they all live and sleep. But last night at ten o'clock nobody seemed to be sleeping. Kids of all ages kept walking in, out, and around, usually accompanied by a few dogs. Everyone is open, smiling, friendly, and obviously quite poor.

Gracias! A Latin American Journal

2

LIMA, PERU, JANUARY 20, 1982

Can we truly live with the poor? Although I live with them and share their life to some extent, I am far from poor. During the noon hour I walk to the rectory in Ciudad de Dios and eat a good meal prepared by a good cook, and one day a week I go to the Maryknoll center house in Miraflores to take a shower, sleep in, and have a day of relaxation.

So my living with the poor hardly makes me poor. Should it be different? Some say yes, some say no. Some feel that to be a priest for the poor, you should be no different from them, others say that such is not realistic or even authentic.

I have been here only one week, and thus am unable to have an opinion, but I know one thing: right now I would be

physically, mentally, and spiritually unable to survive without
the opportunity to break away from it all once in a while. All
the functions of life, which previously hardly required attention, are complicated and time-consuming operations here: washing, cooking, writing, cleaning, and so on. The winds cover
everything with thick layers of dust; water has to be hauled up
in buckets from below and boiled to be drinkable; there is
seldom a moment of privacy, with kids walking in and out all
the time, and the thousands of loud sounds make silence a
faraway dream.

I love living here, but I am also glad that I can escape it for
two hours a day and for one day a week. Living here not only
makes me aware that I have never been poor, but also that my
whole way of being, thinking, feeling, and acting is molded by
a culture radically different from the one I live in now. I am
surrounded by so many safety systems that I would not be
allowed to become truly poor. If I were to become seriously ill,
I would be sent back to the United States and given the best
possible treatment. As soon as my life or health were really
threatened, I would have many people around me willing to
protect me.

At this moment, I feel that a certain realism is necessary.
I am not poor as my neighbors are. I will never be and will
not ever be allowed to be by those who sent me here. I have
to accept my own history and live out my vocation without
denying that history. On the other hand, I realize that the
way of Christ is a self-emptying way. What that precisely
means in my own concrete life will probably remain a lifelong
question.

I am writing all this from my comfortable room in the center
house in Miraflores, where I have a day off. I enjoyed my
shower, I am glad to receive mail and have a dust-free desk on
which to answer it, and I look forward to reading a book,
seeing a movie, and talking to friends about religion, politics,

and "home." But I am also happy that tomorrow I can return to Pablito, Johnny, and Maria and play with them in Pamplona Alta.

Gracias! A Latin American Journal

3

LIMA, PERU, JANUARY 30, 1982

Dust is probably my greatest physical problem here. Wherever I turn, I encounter dust. Walking on the sandy street, I am always surrounded by small clouds of dust, and when a car passes, the dust becomes like a heavy fog that vanishes only slowly. Everything in my room is covered with a layer of fine dust. When I want to write a letter, I first blow the dust away; when I want to drink tea, I have first to wash the dust off the cup; and when I want to go to sleep, I have first to shake the dust from the covers and the sheets. It settles in my hair, ears, and nose. It crawls into my socks, shirts, and pants; and it creeps in between the pages of the books I am reading. Since it is quite humid here, the dust sticks easily to whatever it lands on. This gives me a nearly permanent desire for a shower. Only the realization that the pleasure of feeling clean would probably not last longer than five minutes has helped me to develop a certain indifference to this dustbowl.

Gracias! A Latin American Journal

4

LIMA, PERU, SUNDAY, MARCH 28, 1982

Jesus learned obedience from what he suffered. This means that the pains and struggles of which Jesus became part made him listen more perfectly to God. In and through his sufferings, he came to know God and could respond to God's call. Maybe there are no better words than these to summarize the meaning of the option for the poor. Entering into the suffering of the poor is the way to become obedient, that is, a listener to God. Suffering accepted and shared in love breaks down our selfish defenses and sets us free to accept God's guidance.

After my stay in Bolivia and Peru I think that I have seen, heard, and even tasted the reality of this theology. For me it is no longer an abstract concept. My time with Sophia, Pablo, and their children was an experience that gave me a glimpse of true obedience. Living, working, and playing with them brought me close to a knowledge of God that I had not experienced anywhere before.

But do I really want to know Jesus? Do I really want to listen to him? Do I really want to take up my cross and follow him? Do I really want to dedicate myself to unconditional service?

Gracias! A Latin American Journal

5

GRACIAS AND ADIEU

I look forward to going home tomorrow, to sitting in a comfortable airplane. I like to be welcomed home by friends. I look forward to being back again in my cozy apartment, with my books, my paintings, and my plants. I like showers with hot water, faucets with water you can drink, washing machines that work, and lamps that keep burning. I like cleanliness. But is it there that I will find God?

I look forward to being back at the Trappist monastery in upstate New York, to feeling the gentle silence of the contemplative life, singing the psalmodies in the choir, and celebrating the Eucharist with all the monks in the Abbey church. I look forward to walking again in the spacious fields of the Genesee Valley and driving through the woods of Letchworth Park. But is it there that I will find God?

Or is God in this dusty, dry, cloud-covered city of Lima, in this confusing, unplanned, and often chaotic conglomeration of people, dogs, and houses? Is God perhaps where the hungry kids play, the old ladies beg, and the shoeshine boys pick your pocket?

I surely have to be where God is. I have to become obedient to God, listen to God's voice, and go wherever that voice calls me. Even when I do not like it, even when it is not a way of cleanliness or comfort. Jesus said to Peter: "When you were young you put on your own belt and walked where you liked; but when you grow old you will stretch out your hands, and somebody else will put a belt round you and take you where you would rather not go" (John 21:18). Am I old enough now to be led by the poor, disorganized, unclean, hungry, and uneducated? Everything that is freely given by the God of love. All is grace. Light and water, shelter and food, work and free time, children, parents and grandparents, birth and death—it is all given to us. Why? So that we can say *gracias*, thanks: thanks to God, thanks to each other, thanks to all and everyone.

Gracias! A Latin American Journal

Displacement

The call to community as we hear it from our Lord is the call to move away from the ordinary and proper places. Leave your father and mother. Let the dead bury the dead. Keep your hand on the plow and do not look back. Sell what you own, give the money to the poor, and come follow me (Luke 14:26; 9:60, 62; 18:22). The Gospels confront us with this persistent voice inviting us to move from where it is comfortable, from where we want to stay, from where we feel at home.

Compassion

The paradox of the Christian community is that people are gathered together in voluntary displacement. The togetherness of those who form a Christian community is a being-gathered-in-displacement. According to Webster's dictionary, displacement means to move or to shift from the ordinary or proper place. This becomes a telling definition when we realize the extent to which we are preoccupied with adapting ourselves to the prevalent norms and values of our milieu. We want to be ordinary and proper people who live ordinary and proper lives. There is an enormous pressure on us to do what is ordinary and proper—even the attempt to excel is ordinary and proper—and thus find the satisfaction of general acceptance. This is quite understandable since the ordinary and proper behavior that gives shape to an ordinary and proper life offers us the comforting illusion that things are under control and that everything extraordinary and improper can be kept outside the walls of our self-created fortress.

Compassion

Voluntary displacement as a way of life rather than as a unique event is the mark of discipleship. The Lord, whose compassion we want to manifest in time and place, is indeed the displaced Lord. Paul describes Jesus as the one who voluntarily displaced himself. "His state was divine, yet he did not cling to his equality with God but emptied himself to assume the condition of a slave, and became as we are" (Phil. 2:6-7). A greater displacement cannot be conceived. The mystery of the incarnation is that God assumed the condition of a suffering human being. Thus God became a displaced God to whom nothing human was alien, a God who could fully experience the brokenness of our human condition. . . .

Jesus Christ is the displaced Lord in whom God's compassion becomes flesh. In him we see a life of displacement lived to the fullest. It is in following our displaced Lord that the Christian community is formed.

Compassion

If voluntary displacement is such a central theme in the life of Christ and his followers, must we not begin by displacing ourselves? Probably not. Rather, we must begin to identify in our own lives where displacement is already occurring. We may be dreaming of great acts of displacement while failing to notice in the displacements of our own lives the first indications of God's presence.

Compassion

Displacement
in Our Daily Lives

1

We do not have to look very long or far to find displacements in our lives. Most of us have experienced painful physical displacements. We have moved from one country to another, from West to East, from North to South, from a small town to a large city, from a small, intimate high school to a large, impersonal university, from a playful work milieu to a competitive position; in short, from familiar to very unfamiliar surroundings.

Beyond these physical displacements, our lives may be marked by deeper inner displacements. As the years go by, familiar images and ideas are often pushed out of place. Ways of thinking, which for many years helped us to understand our world, come under criticism and are called old-fashioned or conservative. Rituals and customs that played central roles in the years of our growth and development are suddenly no longer appreciated by our children or neighbors. Family traditions and church celebrations that have given us our most precious memories are suddenly abandoned and even laughed at as sentimental, magical, or superstitious. More than physical displacements, these inner mental and emotional displacements threaten us and give us feelings of being lost or left alone.

Compassion

2

In our modern society, with its increasing mobility and pluriformity, we have become the subjects and often the victims of so many displacements that it is very hard to keep a sense of rootedness, and we are constantly tempted to become bitter and resentful. Our first and often most difficult task, therefore, is to allow these actual displacements to become places where we can hear God's call. It often seems easier to initiate a displacement that we ourselves can control than freely to accept and affirm a displacement that is totally out of our hands.

The main question is, "How can I come to understand and experience God's caring actions in the concrete situation in which I find myself?" This question is difficult because it requires a careful look at the often painful events and experiences of the moment. "Where have I already been asked to leave my father and mother; where have I already been invited to let the dead bury the dead; where am I already challenged to keep my hand on the plow and not look back?" God is always active in our lives. God always calls, always asks us to take up our crosses and follow. But do we see, feel, and recognize that call, or do we keep waiting for the illusory moment when it will really happen? Displacement is not primarily something to do or to accomplish, but something to recognize.

In and through this recognition a conversion can take place, a conversion from involuntary displacement leading to resentment, bitterness, resignation, and apathy, to voluntary displacement that can become an expression of discipleship. We do not have to go after crosses, but we have to take up the crosses that have been ours all along. To follow Jesus, therefore, means first and foremost to discover in our daily lives God's unique vocation for us.

Compassion

Career and Vocation

The word *vocation* comes from the Latin *vocare*, which means "to call." God calls us together into one people fashioned in the image of Christ. It is by Christ's vocation that we are gathered. Here we need to distinguish carefully between vocation and career. In a world that puts such emphasis on success, our concern for a career constantly tends to make us deaf to our vocation. When we are seduced into believing that our career is what counts, we can no longer hear the voice that calls us together; we become so preoccupied with our own plans, projects, or promotions that we push everyone away who prevents us from achieving our goals.

Career and vocation are not mutually exclusive. In fact, our vocation might require us to pursue a certain career. Many people have become excellent doctors, lawyers, technicians, or scientists in response to God's call heard in the community. Quite often, our vocation becomes visible in a specific job, task, or endeavor. But our vocation can never be reduced to these activities. As soon as we think that our careers *are* our vocation, we are in danger of returning to the ordinary and proper places governed by human competition and of using our talents more to separate ourselves from others than to unite ourselves with them in a common life.

A career disconnected from a vocation divides; a career that expresses obedience to our vocation is the concrete way of

making our unique talents available to the community. Therefore, it is not our careers, but our vocation, that should guide
our lives.

Compassion

A vocation is not the exclusive privilege of monks, priests,
religious sisters, or a few heroic lay persons. God calls everyone
who is listening; there is no individual or group for whom
God's call is reserved. But to be effective, a call must be heard,
and to hear it we must continually discern our vocation amidst
the escalating demands of our career.

Compassion

God always calls. To hear that call and allow it to guide our
actions requires discipline in order to prevent ourselves from
remaining or becoming spiritually deaf. There are so many
voices calling for our attention and so many activities distract-
ing us that a serious effort is necessary if we are to become and
remain sensitive to the divine presence in our lives.

When God calls, God gives a new name. Abram became
Abraham, Jacob became Israel, Saul became Paul, and Simon
became Peter. We must search for this new name because the
new name reveals the unique vocation given to us by God.

Compassion

NOTES:

[1]H. C. Rumke, *The Psychology of Unbelief*, New York: Sheed & Ward,
1962.

[2]*Insight*, London: Longmans Green and Co., Ltd., 1957, p. 191.

[3]Benedicta Ward, trans., *The Sayings of the Desert Fathers*, London and
Oxford: Mowfrays, 1975, p. 6.

[4]F. J. Sheed, tran., *Confessions of St. Augustine*, New York: Sheed and
Ward, 1943, p. 178.

[5]Dietrich Bonhoeffer, *Letters and Papers from Prison*, ed. by Eberhard Bethge, New York: Macmillan and Co., 1972, p. 360.

[6]Elie Wiesel, *Souls on Fire, Portraits and Legends of Hasidic Masters*, New York: Random House, 1972, p. 265.

[7]Ibid., p. 269.

[8]Ibid., p. 271.

[9]Ibid., p. 303.

[10]Ibid., p. 298.

[11]Ibid., p. 201.

III

THE ROOTS OF HOPE:
HUMAN DESTINY

How can we come to a creative contact with the
grounding of our own life? Only through a teacher
who can lead us to the source of our
existence by showing us who we
are and, thereby, what
we are to do.

Creative Ministry

Nature
as Revelation

Listen to Autumn

GENESEE ABBEY, OCTOBER 13, 1974

This morning John Eudes spoke in Chapter about autumn as a time of plenitude, a time of fulfillment in which the richness of nature becomes abundantly visible, but also a time in which nature points beyond itself by the fragility of its passing beauty.

He started by reading Psalm 64, which speaks about the beauty of nature. He couldn't have chosen a better day to speak about this psalm. When I walked out I was overwhelmed by the beauty of the landscape unfolding itself before my eyes. Looking out over the Genesee Valley, I was dazzled by the bright colors of the trees. The yellow of the hickory trees, the different shades of red from the maples and oaks, the green of the willows—together they formed a fantastic spectacle. The sky was full of mysterious cloud formations, and just as I walked down to the guest house, the sun's rays burst through the clouds and covered the land with their light, making the corn-fields look like a golden tapestry.

The beauty of the fall is unbelievable in this part of the country. I can only say with the psalmist: "The hills are girded with joy, they shout for joy, yes, they sing."

Two weeks from now the colorful leaves will have whirled to

the ground and the trees will be bare, announcing the coming of winter and snow. It will be only a few months before all the hills will be white and the green of the winter wheat covered with a thick blanket of frozen snow. But then we can remember the rich powers hidden underneath which will show themselves again to those who have the patience to wait.

Genesee Diary

YOU ARE MORE THAN YOU

If we are sensitive to the voice of nature, we might be able to hear sounds from a world where all of humanity and all of nature both find their shape. We will never fully understand the meaning of the sacramental signs of bread and wine when they do not make us realize that the whole of nature is a sacrament pointing to a reality far beyond itself. The presence of Christ in the Eucharist becomes a "special problem" only when we have lost our sense of his presence in all that is, grows, lives, and dies. What happens during a Sunday celebration can only be a real celebration when it reminds us in the fullest sense of what continually happens every day in the world which surrounds us. Bread is more than bread, wine is more than wine: it is God with us—not as an isolated event once a week but as the concentration of a mystery about which all of nature speaks day and night.

Therefore, wasting food is not a sin just because there are still so many hungry people in this world. It is a sin because it is an offense against the sacramental reality of all we eat and drink. But if we become more and more aware of the voices of all that surrounds us and grow in respect and reverence for nature, then we also will be able to truly care for a humanity embedded in nature like a sapphire in a golden ring.

Creative Ministry

Advent: Waiting

1

A BUD SHALL BLOSSOM

"A shoot shall sprout from the stump of Jesse, and from his roots a bud shall blossom. The spirit of the LORD shall rest upon him . . ." (Isa. 11:102).

These words from last night's liturgy have stayed with me during the day. Our salvation comes from something small, tender, and vulnerable, something hardly noticeable. God, who is the Creator of the Universe, comes to us in smallness, weakness, and hiddenness.

I find this a hopeful message. Somehow, I keep expecting loud and impressive events to convince me and others of God's saving power; but over and over again I am reminded that spectacles, power plays, and big events are the ways of the world. Our temptation is to be distracted by them and made blind to the "shoot that shall sprout from the stump."

When I have no eyes for the small signs of God's presence—the smile of a baby, the carefree play of children, the words of encouragement and gestures of love offered by friends—I will always remain tempted to despair.

The small child of Bethlehem, the unknown young man of Nazareth, the rejected preacher, the naked man on the cross, *he* asks for my full attention. The work of our salvation takes place in the midst of a world that continues to shout, scream, and overwhelm us with its claims and promises. But the promise is hidden in the shoot that sprouts from the stump, a shoot that hardly anyone notices.

I remember seeing a film on the human misery and devastation brought by the bomb on Hiroshima. Among all the scenes of terror and despair emerged one image of a man quietly writing a word in calligraphy. All his attention was directed to writing that one word. That image made this gruesome film a hopeful film. Isn't that what God is doing? Writing the divine word of hope in the midst of our dark world?

Gracias! A Latin American Journal

2

WAITING

Waiting, as we see it in the people on the first pages of the Gospels, is waiting with a sense of promise. "Zechariah, your wife Elizabeth is to bear you a son" (Luke 1:13, 31, *JB*). People who wait have received a promise that allows them to wait. They have received something that is at work in them, like a seed that has started to grow. This is very important. We can only really wait if what we are waiting for has already begun for us. So waiting is never a movement from nothing to something. It is always a movement from something to something more. Zechariah, Mary, and Elizabeth were living with a promise that nurtured them, that fed them, and that made them able to stay where they were. And in this way, the promise itself could grow in them and for them.

Secondly, waiting is active. Most of us think of waiting as something very passive, a hopeless state determined by events totally out of our hands. The bus is late? You cannot do anything about it, so you have to sit there and just wait. It is not difficult to understand the irritation people feel when somebody says, "Just wait." Words like that seem to push us into passivity.

But there is none of this passivity in scripture. Those who are waiting are waiting very actively. They know that what they are waiting for is growing from the ground on which they are standing. That's the secret. The secret of waiting is the faith that the seed has been planted, that something has begun. Active waiting means to be present fully to the moment, in the conviction that something is happening where you are and that you want to be present to it. A waiting person is someone who is present to the moment, who believes that this moment is *the moment*.

"A Spirituality of Waiting: Being Alert to
God's Presence in Our Lives," *Weavings*, January 1987

3

WAITING PATIENTLY

A waiting person is a patient person. The word *patience* means the willingness to stay where we are and live the situation out to the fullest in the belief that something hidden there will manifest itself to us. Impatient people are always expecting the real thing to happen somewhere else and therefore want to go elsewhere. The moment is empty. But patient people dare to stay where they are. Patient living means to live actively in the present and wait there. Waiting, then, is not passive. It involves nurturing the moment, as a mother nurtures the child that is growing in her. Zechariah, Elizabeth, and Mary were present to the moment. That is why they could hear the angel.

They were alert, attentive to the voice that spoke to them and said, "Don't be afraid. Something is happening to you. Pay attention."

Ibid., *Weavings*, January 1987

4

WAITING IN HOPE

But there is more. Waiting is open-ended. Open-ended waiting is hard for us because we tend to wait for something very concrete, for something that we wish to have. Much of our waiting is filled with wishes: "I wish that the weather would be better." "I wish that the pain would go." We are full of wishes, and our waiting easily gets entangled in those wishes. For this reason, a lot of our waiting is not open-ended. Instead, our waiting is a way of controlling the future. We want the future to go in a very specific direction, and if this does not happen, we are disappointed and can even slip into despair. That is why we have such a hard time waiting; we want to do the things that will make the desired events take place. Here we can see how wishes tend to be connected with fears.

But Zechariah, Elizabeth, and Mary were not filled with wishes. They were filled with hope. Hope is something very different. Hope is trusting that something will be fulfilled, but fulfilled according to the promises and not just according to our wishes. Therefore, hope is always open-ended. I have found it very important in my own life to let go of my wishes and start hoping. It was only when I was willing to let go of wishes that something really new, something beyond my own expectations, could happen to me.

Ibid., *Weavings*, January 1987

5

WAITING IN OPENNESS

Just imagine what Mary was actually saying in the words, "I am the handmaid of the Lord. Let what you have said be done to me" (Luke 1:38, JB). She was saying, "I don't know what this all means, but I trust that good things will happen." She trusted so deeply that her waiting was open to all possibilities. And she did not want to control them. She believed that when she listened carefully, she could trust what was going to happen.

To wait open-endedly is an enormously radical attitude toward life. So is to trust that something will happen to us that is far beyond our own imaginings. So, too, is giving up control over our future and letting God define our life, trusting that God molds us according to God's love and not according to our fear. The spiritual life is a life in which we wait, actively present to the moment, trusting that new things will happen to us, new things that are far beyond our own imagination, fantasy, or prediction. That, indeed, is a very radical stance toward life in a world preoccupied with control.

Ibid., *Weavings*, January 1987

6

WAITING TOGETHER

How do we wait? One of the most beautiful passages of scripture is Luke 1:39–56, which suggests that we wait together, as did Mary and Elizabeth. What happened when Mary received the words of promise? She went to Elizabeth. Something was happening to Elizabeth as well as to Mary. But how could they live that out?

I find the meeting of these two women very moving because

Elizabeth and Mary came together and enabled each other to wait. Mary's visit made Elizabeth aware of what she was waiting for. The child leapt for joy in her. Mary affirmed Elizabeth's waiting. And then Elizabeth said to Mary, "Blessed is she who believed that the promise made her by the Lord would be fulfilled" (Luke 1:45, JB). And Mary responded, "My soul proclaims the greatness of the Lord" (Luke 1:46, JB). She burst into joy herself. These two women created space for each other to wait. They affirmed for each other that something was happening that was worth waiting for.

I think that is the model of the Christian community. It is a community of support, celebration, and affirmation in which we can lift up what has already begun in us. The visit of Elizabeth and Mary is one of the Bible's most beautiful expressions of what it means to form community, to be together, gathered around a promise, affirming that something is really happening.

That is what prayer is all about. It is coming together around the promise. That is what celebration is all about. It is lifting up what is already there. That is what Eucharist is about. It is saying "Thanks" for the seed that has been planted. It is saying: "We are waiting for the Lord, who has already come."

The whole meaning of the Christian community lies in offering a space in which we wait for what we have already seen. Christian community is the place where we keep the flame alive among us and take it seriously so that it can grow and become stronger in us. In this way we can live with courage, trusting that there is a spiritual power in us that allows us to live in this world without being seduced constantly by despair, lostness, and darkness. . . . Waiting together, nurturing what has already begun, expecting its fulfillment—that is the meaning of marriage, friendship, community, and the Christian life.

Ibid., *Weavings*, January 1987

7

WAITING WITH THE WORD

Our waiting is always shaped by alertness to the word. It is waiting in the knowledge that someone wants to address us. The question is, Are we home? Are we at our address, ready to respond to the doorbell? We need to wait together, to keep each other at home spiritually, so that when the word comes it can become flesh in us. That is why the book of God is always in the midst of those who gather. We read the word so that the word can become flesh and have a whole new life in us.

Ibid., *Weavings*, January 1987

Christmas at
the Abbey

GENESEE ABBEY, DECEMBER 25, 1974

What can I say on a night like this? It is all very small and very large, very close and very distant, very tangible and very elusive. I keep thinking about the Christmas scene that Anthony arranged under the altar. This probably is the most meaningful "crib" I have ever seen. Three small wood-carved figures made in India: a poor woman, a poor man, and a small child between them. The carving is simple, nearly primitive. No eyes, no ears, no mouths, just the contours of the faces. The figures are smaller than a human hand—nearly too small to attract attention at all. But then—a beam of light shines on the three figures and projects large shadows on the wall of the sanctuary. That says it all. The light thrown on the smallness of Mary, Joseph, and the Child projects them as large, hopeful shadows against the walls of our life and our world. While looking at the intimate scene we already see the first outlines of the majesty and glory they represent. While witnessing the most human of human events, I see the majesty of God appearing on the horizon of my existence. While being moved by the gentleness of these three people, I am already awed by the immense greatness of God's love appearing in my world. Without the radiant beam of light shining into the darkness there is little to be seen. I might just pass by these three simple people and continue to walk in darkness. But everything changes with the light.

During these seven months the light has made me see not only the three small figures but also their huge shadows far away. This light makes all things new and reveals the greatness hidden in the small event of this Holy Night. I pray that I will have the strength to keep the light alive in my heart so that I can see and point to the promising shadows appearing on the walls of our world.

Genesee Diary

The Mother of Christ

During dinner I had a very moving conversation with Father André Stoecklin[1] about the importance of Mary in the Christian life. To look at Mary, Father André told me, is to see God's original plan for humanity. In her we see the way God wanted us to be. She is a completely redeemed human being, free from sin and already participating fully in the life of the risen Lord. Mary also shows us how to receive the marvelous gift of God's love, and how to respond to God's redemptive action in our lives. Thus, the closer we come to Mary the better we see the splendor of God's redeemed humanity and the beauty of the redeemed life.

What most struck me in Père André's vision was his conviction that a deep devotion to Mary prevents us from making the Christian life into an ideology. Mary reveals to us the personal quality of God's love as well as the personal quality of a faithful human response.

Mary's full affirmation of God's election made her the Mother of God. God chose to take flesh in the woman who had found favor in God's eyes and had responded to that favor with a full "yes." Her response was not only an initial agreement but a lifelong obedience to God's redemptive presence. In this obedience she followed Jesus in the most perfect way. Her life was a life of always fuller abandonment to the divine will, a total emptying out in faith, a full entering into the darkness of her Son's death. There is no other human being in whom we can see so fully what it means to receive the love of a God who loves us so much that he sent his own Son. She has known more blessing and more suffering than anyone else in all humanity. In her we see most fully what it means to be redeemed.

Thus Mary protects Christianity from becoming a system of ideas, doctrines, opinions, or convictions. She constantly keeps before us that most intimate relationship with her Son. Her complete obedience, radical humility, and unwavering faithfulness show us what a life of following Jesus truly can be. Following Jesus does not mean clinging to an idea or holding on to a principle. It is walking the path of the one who gave his life for his friends and called his followers to do the same. Mary's whole being is in the service of Jesus. She is totally Mother, totally given to letting Jesus be born into this world, not only long ago in Bethlehem, but today and always in the heart of anyone who wants to find God. Her whole being is for Jesus. Seeing Mary always means seeing the Mother of God. Knowing Mary always means knowing the one who gives life to God. It is impossible to encounter Mary truly without being led immediately to Jesus. In her, faith finds its purest expression. She is the woman of faith, who always points away from her self to her Son, the source of our redemption.

Ideologies lead to debates, conflicts, violence, and often war, but faith leads to obedience, humility, faithfulness, and finally peace. Ideologies breed death; faith brings forth life. Mary prevents us from becoming victimized by religious ideology and calls us unceasingly to a life of faith, a faith in him who became flesh in her, a faith that will make it possible for him to become flesh in us too.

Unpublished journal

The Face of Christ

For a week now, I have been trying to write a meditation about the icon of Christ the Savior painted by Andrew Rublev. I have not yet been able to write a word, but in fact have experienced an increasing anxiety. I looked at some books on iconography, studied some articles on Rublev's particular style, read through Ian Wilson's book on the Turin shroud, and let my mind make all sorts of connections—but could not find words for writing. I feel tired, even exhausted, because I have spent much mental energy but have found no way to channel it creatively.

I am gradually realizing that what restrains me is the direct confrontation with the face of Jesus. I have written about Rublev's icon of the Trinity and about the icon of Our Lady of Vladimir. Yet writing about the icon of Christ's sacred face is such an awesome undertaking that I wonder if I can really do it.

This afternoon I just looked at this seemingly indescribable icon. I looked at the eyes of Jesus and saw his eyes looking at me. I choked, closed my eyes, and started to pray. I said, "O my God, how can I write about your face? Please give me the words to say what can be said." I read in the Gospels and realized how much is written there about seeing and being seen, about being blind and receiving new sight, and about eyes—human eyes and the eyes of God.

I know I must write about Rublev's icon of Christ because it touches me more than any icon I have ever seen. I must come to know what happens to me when I look at and pray with it. One thing is certain: I have read enough about it. I must simply be present to it, and pray and look and pray and wait and pray and trust. I hope that the right words will come, because if they do, perhaps many will begin to see with me and be touched by those eyes.

The Road to Daybreak

THE EYES OF CHRIST

What makes seeing Rublev's icon such a profound spiritual experience are the eyes of the Savior. Their gaze is so mysterious and deep that any word which tries to describe them is inadequate. . . . The Christ of Rublev looks directly at us and confronts us with his penetrating eyes. They are large, open eyes accentuated by big brows and deep, round shadows. They are not severe or judgmental but they see all that is. They form the true center of the icon. One could say "Jesus is all eyes." His penetrating look brings to mind the words of the psalmist:

> O Lord, you search me and you know me
> you know my resting and my rising
> you discern my purpose from afar.
> You mark when I walk or lie down,
> all my ways lie open to you. . . .
> O where can I go from your spirit,
> or where can I flee from your face? (Ps. 139:1–3, 7)

These words do not speak of a fear-inspiring omnipresence, but of the loving care of someone who looks after us at all times and in all places. The eyes of Rublev's Jesus are neither sentimental nor judgmental, neither pious nor harsh, neither sweet

nor severe. They are the eyes of God, who sees us in our most
hidden places and loves us with a divine mercy. . . .

Alpatov [writes]: "Before the icon of the Savior [of Rublev]
we feel face to face with him, we look directly into his eyes and
feel a closeness to him."[2]

This face-to-face experience leads us to the heart of the great
mystery of the Incarnation. We can see God and live! As we try
to fix our eyes on the eyes of Jesus we know that we are
seeing the eyes of God. What greater desire is there in the
human heart than to see God? With the apostle Philip our
hearts cry out: "Lord, let us see the Father and then we shall be
satisfied." And the Lord answers:

To have seen me is to have seen the Father. . . .
Do you not believe that I am in the Father
and the Father is in me? (John 14:8–10)

Jesus is the full revelation of God, "the image of the unseen
God" (Col. 1:15). Looking into the eyes of Jesus is the fulfillment of our deepest aspiration.

It is hard to grasp this mystery, but we must try to sense
how the eyes of the Word incarnate truly embrace in their gaze
all there is to be seen. The eyes of Rublev's Christ are the eyes
of the Son of Man and the Son of God described in the book of
Revelation. They are like flames of fire which penetrate the
mystery of the divine. They are the eyes of one whose face is
like the sun shining with all its force, and who is known by the
name: Word of God (see Rev. 1:14, 2:18, 1:16, 19:12–13).
They are the eyes of the one who is "Light from Light, true
God from true God, begotten, not made, one in being with the
Father. . . . through whom all things were made" (Nicene Creed).
Christ is indeed the light in whom all is created. He is the light
of the first day when God spoke the light, divided it from the
darkness, and saw that it was good (Gen. 1:3). Christ is also
the light of the new day shining in the dark, a light that
darkness could not overpower (John 1:5). He is the true light

that enlightens all people (John 1–9). It is awesome to look into the eyes of the only one who truly sees the light, and whose seeing is not different from his being.

But the eyes of Christ which see the splendor of God's light are the same eyes which have seen the lowliness of God's people. . . .

The one who sees unceasingly the limitless goodness of God came to the world, saw it broken to pieces by human sin, and was moved to compassion. The same eyes which see into the heart of God saw the suffering hearts of God's people and wept (see John 11:36). These eyes, which burn like flames of fire penetrating God's own interiority, also hold oceans of tears for the human sorrow of all times and all places. That is the secret of the eyes of Andrew Rublev's Christ. . . .

Through the ruins of our world we see the luminous face of Jesus, a face that no violence, destruction, or war can finally destroy.

Behold the Beauty of the Lord

The Body of Christ

1

SAN FRANCISCO, MAY 28, 1986

Being in California is exciting as well as disturbing to me. It is very hard for me to describe the emotions this world calls forth in me. The pleasant climate, the lush gardens, the splendid trees and flowerbeds, the beautiful views over the bay, the city, the island, and the bridges call forth in me words of praise, gratitude, and joy. But the countless car lots, the intense traffic, the huge advertisements, the new buildings going up all over the place, the smog, the noises, the fastness of living—all of this makes me feel unconnected, lonely, and a little lost.

Maybe the word that summarizes it all is "sensual." All my senses are being stimulated, but with very little grounding, very little history, very little spirit. I keep wondering how my heart can be fed in this world. It seems as if everyone is moving quickly to meet some person or go to some place or some event. But nobody has much of a home. The houses look very temporary. They will probably last a few decades, maybe a century, but then something else will take their place.

The people we meet are very friendly, easygoing, casual, and entertaining; but I keep wondering how to be with them, how to speak with them, how to pray with them. Everything is very open, expressive, and new; but I find myself looking for a space that is hidden, silent, and old. This is a land to which people go in order to be free from tradition, constraints, and an oppressive history. But the price for this freedom is high: individualism, competition, rootlessness, and frequently loneliness and a sense of being lost. When anything goes, everything is allowed, everything is worth a try, then nothing is sacred, nothing venerable, nothing worth much respect. Being young, daring, original, and mobile seems to be the ideal. Old things need to be replaced by new things, and old people are to be pitied.

The body is central. The sun, the beaches, the water, and the lushness of nature open up all the senses. But it is hard to experience the body as the temple of the spirit. That requires a very special discipline. To reach that inner sanctum where God's voice can be heard and obeyed is not easy if you are always called outward. It is not surprising that California has become a place where many spiritual disciplines are being discovered, studied, and practiced. There are many meditation centers—Buddhist, Christian, and nonreligious. More and more people feel a need to discover an inner anchor to keep themselves whole in the midst of the sensual world.

So here I am, somewhat overwhelmed by it all and somewhat confused. How am I to be faithful to Jesus in a world in which having a body is celebrated in so many ways? Jesus is the God who became flesh with us so that we could live with his Spirit. How do I live out this truth in this sun-covered, sensual, nontraditional place?

The Road to Daybreak

2

Today is the feast of Corpus Christi, the Body of Christ. While Edward Malloy, a visiting Holy Cross priest, Don, and I celebrated the Eucharist in the little Chapel of the Holy Cross house in Berkeley, the importance of this feast touched me more than ever. The illness that has severely impaired Don's[3] movements made him, and also me, very conscious of the beauty, intricacy, and fragility of the human body. My visit yesterday to the Castro district, where physical pleasure is so visibly sought and bodily pain so dramatically suffered, reminded me powerfully that I not only *have* a body but also *am* a body. The way one lives in the body, the way one relates to, cares for, exercises, and uses one's own and other people's bodies, is of crucial importance for one's spiritual life.

The greatest mystery of the Christian faith is that God came to us in the body, suffered with us in the body, rose in the body, and gave us his body as food. No religion takes the body as seriously as the Christian religion. The body is not seen as the enemy or as a prison of the Spirit, but celebrated as the Spirit's temple. Through Jesus' birth, life, death, and resurrection, the human body has become part of the life of God. By eating the body of Christ, our own fragile bodies are becoming intimately connected with the risen Christ and thus prepared to be lifted up with him into the divine life. Jesus says, "I am the living bread which has come down from heaven. Anyone who eats this bread will live forever; and the bread that I shall give is my flesh, for the life of the world" (John 6:51).

It is in union with the body of Christ that I come to know the full significance of my own body. My body is much more than a mortal instrument of pleasure and pain. It is a home where God wants to manifest the fullness of the divine glory.

This truth is the most profound basis for the moral life. The abuse of the body—whether it be psychological (e.g., instilling fear), physical (e.g., torture), economic (e.g., exploitation), or sexual (e.g., hedonistic pleasure-seeking)—is a distortion of true human destiny: to live in the body eternally with God. The loving care given to our bodies and the bodies of others is therefore a truly spiritual act, since it leads the body closer toward its glorious existence.

I wonder how I can bring this good news to the many people for whom their body is little more than an unlimited source of pleasure or an unceasing source of pain. The feast of the Body of Christ is given to us to fully recognize the mystery of the body and to help us find ways to live reverently and joyfully in the body in expectation of the risen life with God.

The Road to Daybreak

3

L'ARCHE, FRANCE, GOOD FRIDAY 1986

Good Friday: day of the Cross, day of suffering, day of hope, day of abandonment, day of victory, day of mourning, day of joy, day of endings, day of beginnings.

During the liturgy . . . Père Thomas and Père Gilbert took the huge cross that hangs behind the altar from the wall and held it so that the whole community could come and kiss the dead body of Christ.

They all came, more than four hundred people—handicapped men and women and their helpers and friends. Everybody seemed to know very well what they were doing: expressing their love and gratitude for him who gave his life for them. As they were crowding around the cross and kissing the feet and the head of Jesus, I closed my eyes and could see his sacred body stretched out and crucified upon our planet earth. I saw the immense suffering of humanity during the centuries: people killing each other; people dying from starvation and epidemics; people driven from their homes; people sleeping on the streets of large cities; people clinging to each other in desperation; people flagellated, tortured, burned, and mutilated; people alone in locked flats, in prison dungeons, in labor camps; people craving a gentle word, a friendly letter, a consoling embrace, people—children, teenagers, adults, middle-aged, and elderly— all crying out with an anguished voice: "My God, my God, why have you forsaken us?"

Imagining the naked, lacerated body of Christ stretched out over our globe, I was filled with horror. But as I opened my eyes I saw Jacques, who bears the marks of suffering in his face, kiss the body with passion and tears in his eyes. I saw Ivan carried on Michael's back. I saw Edith coming in her wheel-chair. As they came—walking or limping, seeing or blind, hearing or deaf—I saw the endless procession of humanity gathering around the sacred body of Jesus, covering it with their tears and their kisses, and slowly moving away from it comforted and consoled by such great love. There were sighs of relief; there were smiles breaking through tear-filled eyes; there were hands in hands and arms in arms. With my mind's eye I saw the huge crowds of isolated, agonizing individuals walking away from the cross together, bound by the love they had seen with their own eyes and touched with their own lips. The cross of horror became the cross of hope, the tortured body became the body that gives new life; the gaping wounds became the source of forgiveness, healing, and reconciliation. Père Thomas and Père Gilbert were still holding the cross. The last people came, knelt, and kissed the body, and left. It was quiet, very quiet.

Père Gilbert then gave me a large chalice with the consecrated bread and pointed to the crowd standing around the altar.

I took the chalice and started to move among those whom I had seen coming to the cross, looked at their hungry eyes, and said, "The body of Christ . . . the body of Christ . . . the body of Christ" countless times. The small community became all of humanity, and I knew that all I needed to say my whole life long was "Take and eat. This is the body of Christ."

The Road to Daybreak

The Agony of Christ

1

When we say "Christ has died," we express the truth that all human suffering in time and place has been suffered by the Son of God who also is the Son of all humanity and thus has been lifted up into the inner life of God Himself. There is no suffering—no guilt, shame, loneliness, hunger, oppression, or exploitation, no torture, imprisonment, or murder, no violence or nuclear threat—that has not been suffered by God. There can be no human beings who are completely alone in their sufferings, since God, in and through Jesus, has become Emmanuel, God with us. It belongs to the center of our faith that God is a faithful God, a God who did not want us to ever be alone but who wanted to understand—to stand under—all that is human. The Good News of the Gospel, therefore, is not that God came to take our suffering away, but that God wanted to become part of it.

All of this has been said often before, but maybe not in a way that makes a direct connection with the agony of the world that we witness today. We have to come to the inner knowledge that the agony of the world is God's agony. The agony of women, men, and children during the ages reveals to us the inexhaustible depth of God's agony that we glimpsed in the garden of Gethsemane. The deepest meaning of human history is the gradual unfolding of the suffering of Christ. As long as there is human history, the story of Christ's suffering has not yet been fully told. Every time we hear more about the way human beings are in pain, we come to know more about the immensity of God's love, who did not want to exclude anything human from his experience of being God. God indeed is *Yahweh Rachamin*, the God who carries His suffering people in His womb with the intimacy and care of a mother. This is what Blaise Pascal alluded to when he wrote that Christ is in agony until the end of time.

"Christ of the Americas," *America*,
April 21, 1984

2

The more we try to enter into this mystery the more we will come to see the suffering world as a world hidden in God. Outside of God, human suffering is not only unbearable but cannot even be faced. Understandably, many people say, "I have enough problems of my own, do not bother me with the problems of the world. Just making it from day to day in my family, my town, my work, is enough of a burden. Please do not plague me with the burdens of people in Central America or other places. They only make me feel more angry, more guilty, and more powerless." Outside of God even small burdens can pull us down and destroy our physical, emotional, and spiritual health. Outside of God burdens are to be avoided at all cost. Seeing people's misery and pain outside of God becomes a burden too heavy to carry and makes us feel darkness inside.

But when we come to know the inner connectedness between the world's pain and God's pain, everything becomes radically different. Then we see that in and through Jesus Christ, God has lifted up all human burdens into His own interiority and made them the way to recognize his immense love. Jesus says, "My yoke is easy and my burden light," but Jesus' burden is the burden of all humankind. When we are invited to carry this burden of Jesus, we are invited to carry the burden of the world. The great mystery is that this very burden is a light burden since it is the burden that makes known to us the unlimited love of God.

Here we touch the spiritual dimensions of all social concern. The hunger of the poor, the torture of prisoners, the threat of war in many countries, and the immense human suffering we hear about from all directions can call us to a deeply human response only if we are willing to see in the brokenness of our fellow human beings the brokenness of God, because God's brokenness does not repulse. It attracts by revealing the loving face of the One who came to carry our burdens and to set us free. Seeing the agony of the people then becomes the way of coming to know the love of God, a love that reconciles, heals, and unites.

"Christ of the Americas," *America*, April 21, 1984

COMPASSION: THE OLD MAN AND THE SCORPION

Recently, a friend told me a story that expressed the meaning of compassion better than any explanation I had heard before.

Once there was a very old man who used to meditate early every morning under a large tree on the bank of the Ganges River in India. One morning, having finished his meditation, the old man opened his eyes and saw a scorpion floating helplessly in the strong current of the river. As the scorpion was pulled close to the tree, it got caught in the long tree roots that branched out far into the river. The scorpion struggled frantically to free itself but got more and more entangled in the complex network of the tree roots.

When the old man saw this, he immediately stretched himself onto the extended roots and reached out to rescue the drowning scorpion. But as soon as he touched it, the animal jerked and stung him wildly. Instinctively, the man withdrew his hand, but then, after having regained his balance, he once again stretched himself out along the roots to save the agonized scorpion. But every time the old man came within reach, the scorpion stung him so badly with its poisonous tail that his hands became swollen and bloody and his face distorted by pain.

At that moment, a passerby saw the old man stretched out on the roots struggling with the scorpion and shouted: "Hey, stupid old man. What's wrong with you? Only a fool risks his life for the sake of an ugly, useless creature. Don't you know that you may kill yourself to save that ungrateful animal?"

Slowly the old man turned his head, and looking calmly in the stranger's eyes, he said: "Friend, because it is the nature of the scorpion to sting, why should I give up my own nature to save?"

Well, that's the question: Why should we give up our nature to be compassionate even when we get stung in a biting, stinging world? The story about the old man and the scorpion holds out a great challenge to a society in which we are made to believe that mutual struggle dominates the process of human development. It challenges us to show that to embrace is more human than to reject, that to kiss is more human than to bite, to behold more human than to stare, to be friends more human than to be rivals, to make peace more human than to make war—in short, that compassion is more human than strife.

"Compassion," *America*, March 13, 1976

THE HANDS AND FEET OF CHRIST

FRANCE, APRIL 3, 1986

Jesus' hands and feet were not just anyone's hands and feet, but the signs of his real bodily presence. They were the hands and feet of Jesus marked with the wounds of his Crucifixion. It is of great spiritual importance that Jesus made himself known to his disciples by showing them his wounded body. The resurrection had not taken his wounds away, but, rather, they had become part of his glory. They had become glorified wounds.

Jesus is the Lord who came to save us by dying for us on the Cross. The wounds in Jesus' glorified body remind us of the way in which we are saved. But they also remind us that our own wounds are much more than roadblocks on our way to God. They show us our own unique way to follow the suffering Christ, and they are destined to become glorified in our resurrected life. Just as Jesus was identified by his wounds, so are we.

This mystery is hard to grasp, but it is of the greatest importance in helping us to deal with our own brokenness.

When I feel lonely, forgotten, rejected, or despised, I can easily be tempted to respond to these painful experiences with anger, resentment, and a desire for revenge. Much violence in our world is a desperate acting-out of that wounded inner self. But if I am willing to claim my woundedness as my unique way to the resurrection, then I may start caring for my wounds, knowing that they will identify me in my eternal life in God. What does this "caring for my wounds" mean? It means acknowledging them as revelations of my unique way of being human, listening to them as teachers who help me find my own way to holiness, sharing them as a source of consolation and comfort, and allowing others to pour oil on them and bind them in times of great pain.

Thus I proclaim that my wounds are not causes for embarrassment, but the source of a joyful acknowledgment of my unique vocation to journey with Jesus through suffering to the glory of God.

Unpublished journal

The Human Journey: Aging and Dying

AGING: THE FULFILLMENT OF LIFE

We all age and so fulfill the cycle of our lives. This is what the large wagon wheel reclining against the old birch in the white snow teaches us by its simple beauty. No one of its spokes is more important than the others, but together they make the circle full and reveal the hub as the core of its strength. The more we look at it, the more we come to realize that we have only one life cycle to live, and that living it is the source of our greatest joy.

The restful accomplishment of the old wheel tells us the story of life. Entering into the world we are what we are given, and for many years thereafter parents and grandparents, brothers and sisters, friends and lovers keep giving to us—some more, some less, some hesitantly, some generously. When we can finally stand on our own feet, speak our own words, and express our own unique self in work and love, we realize how much is given to us. But while reaching the height of our cycle, and saying with a great sense of confidence, "I really am," we sense that to fulfill our life we now are called to become parents and grandparents, brothers and sisters, teachers, friends, and lovers ourselves, and to give to others, so that when we leave this world we can be what we have given.

The wagon wheel reminds us that the pains of growing old are worthwhile. The wheel turns from ground to ground but not without moving forward. Although we have only one life cycle to live, although it is only a small part of human history which we will cover, to do this gracefully and carefully is our greatest vocation. Indeed, we go from dust to dust, we move up to go down, we grow to die, but the first dust does not have to be the same as the second, the going down can become the moving on, and death can be made into our final gift.

Aging is the turning of the wheel, the gradual fulfillment of the life cycle in which receiving matures in giving and living makes dying worthwhile.

Aging

CARING

What does it mean to care? . . . The word *care* finds its roots in the Gothic "Kara," which means "lament." The basic meaning of care is to grieve, to experience sorrow, to cry out with. I am very much struck by this background of the word *care* because we tend to look at caring as an attitude of the strong toward the weak, of the powerful toward the powerless, of the haves toward the have-nots. And, in fact, we feel quite uncomfortable with an invitation to enter into someone's pain before doing something about it.

Still, when we honestly ask ourselves which persons in our lives mean the most to us, we often find that it is those who, instead of giving much advice, solutions, or cures, have chosen rather to share our pain and touch our wounds with a gentle and tender hand. The friend who can be silent with us in a moment of despair or confusion, who can stay with us in an hour of grief and bereavement, who can tolerate not-knowing, not-curing, not-healing and face with us the reality of our power-lessness, that is the friend who cares. . . .

Therefore, to care means first of all to be present to each other. From experience you know that those who care for you become present to you. When they listen, they listen to you. When they speak, you know they speak to you. And when they ask questions, you know it is for your sake and not for their own. Their presence is a healing presence because they accept you on your terms, and they encourage you to take your own life seriously and to trust your own vocation.

Our tendency is to run away from the painful realities or to try to change them as soon as possible. But cure without care makes us into rulers, controllers, manipulators, and prevents a real community from taking shape. Cure without care makes us preoccupied with quick changes, impatient and unwilling to share each other's burden. And so cure can often become offending instead of liberating. It is therefore not so strange that cure is not seldom refused by people in need.

Out of Solitude

AGING: CARE AND THE ELDERLY

The challenge of care for the elderly is that we are called to make our own aging self the main instrument of our healing. . . .

Aging

There can hardly be a better image of caring than that of the artist who brings new life to people by an honest and fearless self-portrait. Rembrandt painted his sixty-three self-portraits not just as "a model for studies in expression" but as "a search for the spiritual through the channel of his innermost personality." Rembrandt felt that he had to enter into his own self, into his dark cellars as well as into his light rooms if he really wanted to penetrate the mystery of human interiority. Rembrandt realized that what is most personal is most universal. While growing in age he was more and more able to touch the core of the human experience, in which individuals in their misery can recognize themselves and find "courage and new youth." We will never be able to really care if we are not willing to paint and repaint constantly our self-portrait, not as a morbid self-preoccupation, but as a service to those who are searching for some light in the midst of the darkness.

Aging

To care one must offer one's own vulnerable self to others as a source of healing. To care for the aging, therefore, means first of all to enter into close contact with your own aging self, to sense your own time, and to experience the movements of your own life cycle. From this aging self, healing can come forth and others can be invited to cast off the paralyzing fear for their future. As long as we think that caring means only being nice and friendly to old people, paying them a visit, bringing them a flower, or offering them a ride, we are apt to forget how much more important it is for us to be willing and able to be present to those we care for.

And how can we be fully present to the elderly when we are hiding from our own aging? How can we listen to their pains when their stories open wounds in us that we are trying to cover up? How can we offer companionship when we want to keep our own aging self out of the room, and how can we gently touch the vulnerable spots in old people's lives when we have armored our own vulnerable self with fear and blindness? Only as we enter into solidarity with the aging and speak out of common experience can we help others to discover the freedom of old age. By welcoming the elderly into our aging self we can be good hosts and healing can take place.

Aging

DYING

Suzuki says: "After some years we will die. If we just think it is the end of our life, this will be the wrong understanding. But, on the other hand, if we think that we do not die, this is also wrong. We die, and we do not die. This is the right understanding."[4]

Genesee Diary

Death is part of a much greater and much deeper event, the fullness of which we cannot comprehend, but of which we know that it is a life-bringing event.

A Letter of Consolation

When Jesus said that if a grain of wheat dies it will yield a rich harvest, he not only spoke about his own death but indicated the new meaning he would give to our death.

A Letter of Consolation

BEFRIENDING DEATH

It seems indeed important that we face death before we are in any real danger of dying and reflect on our mortality before all our conscious and unconscious energy is directed to the struggle to survive. It is important to be prepared for death, very important; but if we start thinking about it only when we are terminally ill, our reflections will not give us the support we need. . . . Once you have reached the top of the mountain, it does not make much difference at which point on the way down you take a picture of the valley—as long as you are not in the valley itself.

I think, then, that our first task is to befriend death. I like that expression "to befriend." I first heard it used by Jungian analyst James Hillman when he attended a seminar I taught on Christian spirituality at Yale Divinity School. He emphasized the importance of "befriending:" befriending your dreams, befriending your shadow, befriending your unconscious. He made it convincingly clear that in order to become full human beings, we have to claim the totality of our experience; we come to maturity by integrating not only the light but also the dark side of our story into our selfhood. That made a lot of sense to me, since I am quite familiar with my own inclination, and that of others, to avoid, deny, or suppress the painful side of life, a tendency that always leads to physical, mental, or spiritual disaster.

And isn't death, the frightening unknown that lurks in the depths of our unconscious minds, like a great shadow that we perceive only dimly in our dreams? Befriending death seems to be the basis of all other forms of befriending. I have a deep sense, hard to articulate, that if we could really befriend death, we would be free people. So many of our doubts and hesitations, ambivalences and insecurities, are bound up with our deep-seated fear of death, that our lives would be significantly different if we could relate to death as a familiar guest instead of a threatening stranger. . . . Fear of death often drives us into death, but by befriending death we can face our mortality and choose life freely.

But how do we befriend death? . . . I think love—deep, human love—does not know death. . . . Real love says, "Forever." Love will always reach out toward the eternal. Love comes from that place within us where death cannot enter. Love does not accept the limits of hours, days, weeks, months, years, or centuries. Love is not willing to be imprisoned by time. . . .

The same love that reveals the absurdity of death also allows us to befriend death. The same love that forms the basis of our grief is also the basis of our hope; the same love that makes us cry out in pain also must enable us to develop a liberating intimacy with our own most basic brokenness. Without faith, this must sound like a contradiction. But our faith in Jesus, whose love overcame death and who rose from the grave on the third day, converts this contradiction into a paradox, the most healing paradox of our existence.

A Letter of Consolation

I am constantly struck by the fact that those who are most detached from life, those who have learned through living that there is nothing and nobody in this life to cling to, are the really creative people. They are free to move constantly away from the familiar, safe places and can keep moving forward to new, unexplored areas of life.

A Letter of Consolation

DEATH

GENESEE ABBEY, JULY 31, 1974

I remember very vividly my hitchhike travels through the dark, melancholy hills of Northern Ireland. I wrote articles about the storytellers of Donegal for the Dutch newspapers and, while Kerry and Killarney left hardly any memories in my mind, Donegal I will never forget.

There was something somber but also profound and even holy about Donegal. The people were like the land. I still see vividly the simple funeral of a Donegal farmer. The priest and a few men carried the humble coffin to the cemetery. After the coffin was put into the grave, the men filled the grave with sand and covered it again with the patches of grass which had been laid aside. Two men stamped with their boots on the sod so that it was hardly possible to know that this was a grave. Then one of the men took two pieces of wood, bound them together in the form of a cross, and stuck it in the ground. Everyone made a quick sign of the cross and left silently. No words, no solemnity, no decoration. Nothing of that. But it never has been made so clear to me that someone was dead, not asleep but dead, not passed away but dead, not laid to rest but dead, plain dead. When I saw those two men stamping on the ground in which they had buried their friend, I knew that for these farmers of Donegal there were no funeral-home games to play. But their realism became a transcendent realism by the simple, unadorned wooden cross saying that where death is affirmed, hope finds its roots. "Unless a wheat grain falls on the ground and dies, it remains only a single grain; but if it dies, it yields a rich harvest" (John 12:24).

Genesee Diary

AFTER DEATH:
WAITING FOR THE SPIRIT
OF TRUTH

In the fall of 1978 Laurent and Maria Nouwen flew from Holland to visit their son, Henri, at Yale University, where he was teaching. They had barely arrived when Maria developed symptoms of fatigue and loss of appetite. Alarmed, Henri lost no time in getting her to a doctor. The diagnosis struck like lightning: cancer. She was to return to Holland immediately for emergency surgery.

Nouwen followed his parents back to Holland, where he remained at his mother's bedside until her death, October 9, six days after surgery.

Soon afterward he circulated among friends his memories of her last days and the experience of his bereavement. Touched by the account, friends pressed for publication. Nouwen yielded. The result: In Memoriam, published two years later.

Following is an excerpt from the book.

In a society which is much more inclined to help you hide your pain than to grow through it, it is necessary to make a very conscious effort to mourn. The days when those in grief wore dark clothes and abstained from public life for many months are gone. But I felt that without a very explicit discipline, I might be tempted to return to "normal" and so forget my mother even against my will.

But I know that I must not forget, that I must remember her even if remembering brings with it pain, sorrow, and sadness. The disciples of Jesus kept themselves isolated from the people for forty days, trying to comprehend what had happened. This long period of mourning was necessary before they were able to receive the Spirit. Only after this long and painful grief were they able to receive the great consolation that their Lord had promised them. For it was only after they had given up clinging to their Lord that his Spirit could descend into their hearts.

If Mother's agony and death were indeed an agony and death with Christ, should I not then hope that she would also participate in the sending of the Spirit? The deeper I entered into my own grief, the more I became aware that something new was about to be born, something that I had not known before. I began to wonder if Jesus does not send his Spirit every time someone with whom we are connected by bonds of love leaves us.

To forget Mother would be like forbidding her to send the Spirit to me, refusing to let her lift me up to a new level of insight and understanding of my life. I started to feel the power of Jesus' words: "It is for your own good that I am going, because unless I go, the Advocate [the Spirit] will not come to you; but if I do go, I will send him to you. . . . When the Spirit of truth comes he will lead you to the complete truth" (John 16:7, 13).

Is it for my own good that Jesus died, that my friends and relatives died, that my mother died? Am I able to affirm with my entire being that in and through Christ, death has become the way by which the Spirit of truth comes to us? Must I grieve and mourn so that I will be ready to receive the Spirit when he comes?

These questions became very real to me in those confusing weeks after Mother's death. I said to myself, "This is a time of waiting for the Spirit of truth to come, and woe unto me if, by forgetting her, I prevent her from doing God's work in me." I sensed that something much more than a filial act of remembering was at stake, much more than an honoring of my dead mother, much more than a holding on to her beautiful example. Very specifically, what was at stake was the life of the Spirit in me. To remember her does not mean telling her story over and over again to my friends, nor does it mean pictures on the wall or a stone on her grave; it does not even mean constantly thinking about her. No. It means making her a participant in God's ongoing work of redemption by allowing her to dispel in me a little more of my darkness and lead me a little closer to the light. In these weeks of mourning she died in me more and more every day, making it impossible for me to cling to her as my mother. Yet by letting her go I did not lose her. Rather, I found that she is closer to me than ever. In and through the Spirit of Christ, she indeed is becoming a part of my very being.

In Memoriam

The friends of Jesus saw him and heard him only a few times after that Easter morning, but their lives were completely changed. What seemed to be the end proved to be the beginning; what seemed to be a cause for fear proved to be a cause for courage; what seemed to be defeat proved to be victory; and what seemed to be the basis for despair proved to be the basis for hope. Suddenly a wall becomes a gate, and although we are not able to say with much clarity or precision what lies beyond that gate, the tone of all that we do and say on our way to the gate changes drastically.

A Letter of Consolation

Eternity is born in time, and every time someone dies whom we have loved dearly, eternity can break into our mortal existence a little bit more.

A Letter of Consolation

The Last Hours of Christ

1

A PERSONAL STORY

In the passion and resurrection of Jesus we see God as a waiting God. That is the second aspect of waiting that affects our whole spiritual life. So it is to the end of Jesus' life that I want to turn our attention. Let me start with a story.

I was invited to visit a friend who was very sick. He was a man about fifty-three years old who had lived a very active, useful, faithful, creative life. Actually, he was a social activist who had cared deeply for people. When he was fifty he found out he had cancer, and the cancer became more and more severe.

When I came to him, he said to me, "Henri, here I am lying in this bed, and I don't even know how to think about being sick. My whole way of thinking about myself is in terms of action, in terms of doing things for people. My life is valuable because I've been able to do many things for many people. And suddenly, here I am, passive, and I can't do anything anymore." And he said to me, "Help me to think about this situation in a new way. Help me to think about my not being able to do anything anymore so I won't be driven to despair. Help me to understand what it means that now all sorts of people are doing things to me over which I have no control."

As we talked I realized that he and many others were constantly thinking, "How much can I still do?" Somehow this man had learned to think about himself as a man who was worth what he was doing. And so when he got sick, his hope seemed to rest on the idea that he might get better and return to what he had been doing. I realized, too, that this way of thinking was hopeless because the man had cancer and was going to get worse and worse. He would die soon. If the spirit of this man was dependent on how much he would still be able to do, what did I have to say to him?

It was in the context of these thoughts that together we read a book called *The Stature of Waiting* by British author V. H. Vanstone[5]. Vanstone writes about Jesus' agony in the Garden of Gethsemane and the events that followed. I want to draw on this powerful book in what follows. It helped my friend and me struggle together to understand better what it means to move from action to passion.

"A Spirituality of Waiting," *Weavings*,
January 1987

2

HANDED OVER

The central phrase in the story of Jesus' arrest is one I never thought much about. It is "to be handed over." That is what happened in Gethsemane. Jesus was handed over. Some translations say that Jesus was "betrayed," but the Greek says "to be handed over." Judas handed Jesus over (see Mark 14:10). But the remarkable thing is that the same word is used not only for Judas but also for God. God did not spare Jesus, but handed him over to benefit us all (see Rom. 8:32).

So this phrase, "to be handed over," plays a central role in the
life of Jesus. Indeed, this drama of being handed over divides
the life of Jesus radically in two. The first part of Jesus' life is
filled with activity. Jesus takes all sorts of initiatives. He speaks;
he preaches; he heals; he travels. But immediately after Jesus is
handed over, he becomes the one to whom things are being
done. He's being arrested; he's being led to the high priest; he's
being taken before Pilate; he's being crowned with thorns; he's
being nailed on a cross. Things are being done to him over
which he has no control. That is the meaning of passion—
being the recipient of other people's initiatives.

Ibid., *Weavings*, January 1987

3

GOD'S WAITING

It is important for us to realize that when Jesus says "It is
accomplished" (John 19:30), he does not simply mean "I have
done all the things I wanted to do." He also means "I have
allowed things to be done to me that needed to be done to me
in order for me to fulfill my vocation." Jesus does not fulfill his
vocation in action only, but also in passion. He doesn't fulfill
his vocation just by doing the things the Father sent him to do,
but also by letting things be done to him that the Father allows
to be done to him, by receiving other people's initiatives.

Passion is a kind of waiting—waiting for what other people
are going to do. Jesus went to Jerusalem to announce the good
news to the people of that city. And Jesus knew that he was
going to put a choice before them: Will you be my disciple, or
will you be my executioner? There is no middle ground here.
Jesus went to Jerusalem to put people in a situation where they

had to say yes or no. That is the great drama of Jesus' passion: he had to wait upon how people were going to respond. How would they come? To betray him or to follow him? In a way, his agony is not simply the agony of approaching death. It is also the agony of having to wait. It is the agony of a God who depends on us for how God is going to live out the divine presence among us. It is the agony of the God who, in a very mysterious way, allows us to decide how God will be God. Here we glimpse the mystery of God's incarnation. God became human so that we could act upon God and God could be the recipient of our responses.

Ibid., *Weavings*, January 1987

4

OUR WAITING

All action ends in passion because the response to our action is out of our hands. That is the mystery of work, the mystery of love, the mystery of friendship, the mystery of community—they always involve waiting. And that is the mystery of Jesus' love. God is revealed in Jesus as the one who waits for our response. Precisely in that waiting the intensity of God's love is revealed to us. If God forced us to love, we would not really be lovers.

All these insights into Jesus' passion were very important in the discussions with my friend. He realized that after much hard work he had to wait. He came to see that his vocation as a human being would be fulfilled not just in his actions but also in his passion. And together we began to understand that precisely in this waiting the glory of God and our new life both become visible.

Ibid., *Weavings*, January 1987

The Glory of Christ

1

Resurrection is not just life after death. First of all, it is the life that bursts forth in Jesus' passion, in his waiting. The story of Jesus' suffering reveals that the resurrection is breaking through even in the midst of the passion. A crowd led by Judas came to Gethsemane. "Then Jesus . . . came forward and said to them, 'Whom do you seek?' They answered him, 'Jesus of Nazareth.' Jesus said to them, 'I am he.' . . . When he said to them 'I am he,' they drew back and fell to the ground. Again he asked them, 'Whom do you seek?' And they said, 'Jesus of Nazareth.' Jesus answered, 'I told you that I am he; so, if you seek me, let these men go' " (John 18:4–8, *RSV*).

Precisely when Jesus is being handed over into his passion, he manifests his glory. "Whom do you seek? . . . I am he" are words which echo all the way back to Moses and the burning bush: "I am the one. I am who I am" (see Ex. 3:1–6). In Gethsemane, the glory of God manifested itself, and they fell flat on the ground. Then Jesus was handed over. But already in the handing over we see the glory of God who hands himself over to us. God's glory revealed in Jesus embraces passion as well as resurrection.

"The Son of Man," Jesus says, "must be lifted up as Moses lifted up the serpent in the desert, so that everyone who believes may have eternal life in him" (John 3:14–15, *JB*). He is lifted up as a passive victim, so the Cross is a sign of desolation. And he is lifted up in glory, so the Cross becomes at the same time a sign of hope. Suddenly we realize that the glory of God, the divinity of God, bursts through in Jesus' passion precisely when he is most victimized. So new life becomes visible not only in the resurrection on the third day, but already in the passion, in the being handed over. Why? Because it is in the passion that the fullness of God's love shines through. It is supremely a waiting love, a love that does not seek control.

When we allow ourselves to feel fully how we are being acted upon, we can come in touch with a new life that we were not even aware was there. This was the question my sick friend and I talked about constantly. Could he taste the new life in the midst of his passion? Could he see that in his being acted upon by the hospital staff he was already being prepared for a deeper love? It was a love that had been underneath all the action, but he had not tasted it fully. So together we began to see that in the midst of our suffering and passion, in the midst of our waiting, we can already experience the resurrection.

"A Spirituality of Waiting," *Weavings*, January 1987

2

If we look at our world, how much are we really in control? Isn't our life in large part passion? Of course, we are active, but the margin in which we are active is much smaller than the margin in which we are acted upon by people, events, the culture in which we live, and many other factors beyond our control. This becomes especially clear when we notice how many people are handicapped, chronically ill, elderly, or restricted economically.

It seems that there are more and more people in our society who have less and less influence on the decisions that affect their own existence. Therefore, it becomes increasingly important to recognize that the largest part of our existence involves waiting in the sense of being acted upon. But the life of Jesus tells us that not to be in control is part of the human condition. His vocation was fulfilled not just in action but also in passion, in waiting.

Imagine how important that message is for people in our world. If it is true that God in Jesus Christ is waiting for our response to divine love, then we can discover a whole new perspective on how to wait in life. We can learn to be obedient people who do not always try to go back to the action but who recognize the fulfillment of our deepest humanity in passion, in waiting. If we can do this, I am convinced that we will come in touch with the glory of God and our own new life. Then our service to others will include our helping them see the glory breaking through, not only where they are active but also where they are being acted upon. And so the spirituality of waiting is not simply our waiting for God. It is also participating in God's own waiting for us and in that way coming to share in the deepest purity of love, which is God's love.

Ibid., *Weavings*, January 1987

THE BODILY RESURRECTION OF CHRIST

1

FRANCE, FEBRUARY 28, 1986

Today I received from Bob Heller, my editor at Doubleday, James Bentley's new book, *Secrets of Mount Sinai* (Doubleday, 1986). I started to read it and soon became so fascinated I could hardly put it down. It tells the shocking and highly revelatory story of how the German Protestant scripture scholar Constantin von Tischendorf discovered and published in facsimile the "Codex Sinaiticus," one of the world's oldest Bible texts. It reads like a suspense novel in which genius, religious prejudice, rivalry, ambition, manipulation, deceit, and an enormous amount of European arrogance played a role in bringing this most precious manuscript from St. Catherine's Monastery at Mount Sinai to Russia and from there to the British Museum.

The energy, willpower, and desire for scholarly prestige with which biblical scholars in the eighteenth century did their work are astounding. More astounding is the disdain they felt for the monks who for centuries had guarded the manuscript in which they were interested.

With the mind of a German scholar, Tischendorf judged and condemned his hosts at Mount Sinai. Tischendorf and most of many earlier Protestant visitors to St. Catherine's Monastery never tried to enter into the contemplative tradition they witnessed. Bentley writes: "They took their own religious superiority for granted." This despising of the monks made Tischendorf and others feel that the monks were not worthy of the manuscripts. It gave them an excuse to use the most base methods to get the manuscripts and transport them to the "enlightened West."

Unpublished journal

2

THE MOST PROFOUND BASIS FOR THE SACREDNESS OF ALL HUMAN FLESH

SUNDAY, MARCH 2, 1986

Bentley's book about the secrets of Mount Sinai concludes with a refutation of the bodily resurrection of Jesus. He believes that an alternative, more "spiritual" understanding of the resurrection was successfully suppressed by the defenders of the bodily resurrection. As for the general resurrection of the dead, he cites the *Letter to Rheuigos*, a recently discovered text from Nag Hammadi, whose author, says Bentley, "assumes that there is no resurrection of the physical body. Rather, human reason, or *nous*, can escape from the world and the body into primeval nakedness. In this, Christians are following the way of Jesus."

Bentley also feels that the notion of the resurrection of Jesus as it existed in the minds of St. Basil, St. Gregory of Nyssa, St. Maximus the Confessor, and St. John Klimakos "is far more spiritual than the concept of a resurrected corpse with which many once erroneously supposed St. Mark ended his Gospel." Bentley agrees with his fellow Anglican priest Don Cupitt that the apostles' faith that Jesus was still alive was not based on "meetings with a physically risen Lord," but "arose from deep reflection, theological and personal, on what he had done while he walked on earth" before the Crucifixion (Bentley).

As I read this I discovered how different my own thinking about the resurrection is. It is of crucial importance to affirm the bodily resurrection of Jesus. If the resurrection is only a spiritual event, as the gnostic writers see it, why then did the women find the grave empty? It was clear that his body was no longer there. Even Mark wants to say that. And the resurrection stories of all the other evangelists keep stressing that Jesus rose with his body. He walked, drank, and could be touched. But they also stressed that he was not a resurrected corpse but had a body not subject to the human boundaries of time and space. It was a body marked with the signs of his previous life—the wounds—but also a body that was different from the flesh and bones that were nailed to the Cross. It was his own body but no longer subject to the ordinary laws of nature.

One can speak about a spiritual body to indicate continuity as well as difference in regard to the body of the itinerant preacher of Nazareth. But to say that the stories about the appearances of Jesus to his disciples are written to accommodate

the human weakness which asks for proof is in drastic contradiction to all that the Gospels of Matthew, Luke, and John
stand for.

Why is all of this so important? One reason is that the bodily
resurrection of Jesus is the basis for the Christian attitude
toward the human body. If the body is only a prison room from
which we must be freed, then care for the hungry, the sick, the
dying, prisoners, and refugees can no longer be seen as care for
the body that is called to share in the glory of God.

The bodily resurrection of Jesus is the most profound basis
for the sacredness of all human flesh and the most compelling
argument for reverencing all forms of life. For Jean Vanier at
l'Arche, the bodily resurrection of Jesus is the most precious of
Christian truths. I can see why. Daily physical contact with
severely handicapped people has put him in touch with the
mystery of the human body. Their often very distorted bodies
are not simply temporary dwelling places of an eternal spirit,
but the sacred ground of the resurrected life. Washing, dress-
ing, feeding, and supporting deeply handicapped people is a holy
vocation when we know that their bodies, like ours, are destined
to share in the resurrection of Jesus.

I am not suggesting that without belief in the bodily resurrection of Jesus there can be no good care of the human body, but
I do say that the bodily resurrection does give this care its most
sacred meaning.

None of this is meant to be a "proof" for the bodily resurrection. But sometimes it is good to realize the full implications of
such a truth while others are busy questioning its biblical basis.
I often wonder if the Christian community could have shown so
many ways of caring for the human body without the underly-
ing conviction that the mortal human body is the seed of the
risen body destined for eternal life.

Unpublished journal

I AM THE GLORY OF GOD

GENESEE ABBEY, JULY 15, 1974

When I went to see John Eudes today my head seemed so filled with questions that I wondered how we could focus a little bit and bring some order into the chaos of concerns.

When I left I had the feeling that many things had indeed come together by focusing on the glory of God. The question "How to live for the glory of God and not for your own glory?" has become very important to me. . . . Yes, there is a great temptation to make even God the object of my passion and to search for God not for God's glory but for the glory that can be derived from smart manipulation of godly ideas.

John Eudes wasn't very surprised by my worries. He welcomed them as important enough to worry about, to think about, to live through.

How to dispel the passions that make us manipulate instead of worship? Well, the first thing to realize is that you *are* the glory of God. In Genesis you can read: "Yahweh God fashioned man of dust from the soil. Then he breathed into his nostrils a breath of life, and thus man became a living being" (Gen. 2:7). We live because we share God's breath, God's life, God's glory. The question is not so much "How to live for the glory of God?" but "How to live who we are, how to make true our deepest self?"

With a smile John Eudes said, "Take this as your koan[6]: 'I am the glory of God.' Make that thought the center of your meditation so that it slowly becomes not only a thought but a living reality. You are the place where God chose to dwell, you are the *topos tou theou* (God's place) and the spiritual life is nothing more or less than to allow that space to exist where God can dwell, to create the space where God's glory can manifest itself.

In your meditation you can ask yourself, 'Where is the glory of God? If the glory of God is not there where I am, where else can it be?' "

Genesee Diary

A Prayer to Christident

Dear Lord, help me keep my eyes on you. You are the incarnation of Divine Love, you are the expression of God's infinite compassion, you are the visible manifestation of the Father's holiness. You are beauty, goodness, gentleness, forgiveness, and mercy. In you all can be found. Outside of you nothing can be found. Why should I look elsewhere or go elsewhere? You have the words of eternal life, you are food and drink, you are the Way, the Truth, and the Life. You are the light that shines in the darkness, the lamp on the lampstand, the house on the hilltop. You are the perfect Icon of God. In and through you I can see and find my way to the Heavenly Father. O Holy One, Beautiful One, Glorious One, be my Lord, my Savior, my Redeemer, my Guide, my Consoler, my Comforter, my Hope, my Joy, and my Peace. To you I want to give all that I am. Let me be generous, not stingy or hesitant. Let me give you all—all I have, think, do, and feel. It is yours, O Lord. Please accept it and make it fully your own. Amen.

A Cry for Mercy

NOTES:

[1]*Editor's note.* Father André Stoecklin: Superior of the community of the Servants of Jesus and Mary, a small French religious community of men founded in 1930 by Father Jean Edouard Lamy and relocated in 1941 among the ruins of the old Cistercian Abbey of Our Lady of Ourscamp.

[2]M. Alpatov, Andrew Rublev, Moscow: *Izobrazitel'noe Isskustvo*, 1972.

[3]*Editor's note.* Don McNeill, Director of the Center for Social Concerns at the University of Notre Dame. A close friend of Nouwen's and a coauthor with him of *Compassion*. Although suffering from a muscular disease at the time, he has since returned to his post at Notre Dame.

[4]Shunryu Suzuki, *Zen Mind, Beginner's Mind*, ed. Trudy Dixon, New York and Tokyo: Weatherill, 1970, p. 18.

[5]V. H. Vanstone, *The Stature of Waiting*, New York: Winston-Seabury Press, 1983.

[6]*Editor's note.* William Johnston, S.J., defines *koan* thus: "(Japanese), paradoxical problem pointing to ultimate truth. It is meaningless to the rational intellect and can be solved only by awakening a deeper level of the mind beyond discursive thought." (*Silent Music*, New York: Harper and Row, 1974, p. 176.)

IV

HOPE IN
A NUCLEAR AGE

I open one door and find 100 closed doors.

—ANTONIO PORCHIA
The Wounded Healer

The Predicament of Humanity in a Nuclear Age

1

JESSIE'S SPARROW

L'ARCHE, FRANCE, AUGUST 23, 1985

Yesterday John Fraser, the European correspondent of the *Globe and Mail*, one of Canada's national newspapers, came to visit Madame Vanier. I was invited for tea. We talked about the people of China, Tibet and the Dalai Lama, the Catholic Church in the Philippines and North Korea, and the Pope's recent visit to Holland. . . .

Among all his stories about world events, John told us a small story about his daughter Jessie. It is this story I will remember most:

> One morning when Jessie was four years old, she found a dead sparrow in front of the living room window. The little bird had killed itself by flying into the glass. When Jessie saw the dead bird she was both deeply disturbed and very intrigued. She asked her father: "Where is the bird now?" John said he didn't know. "Why did it die?" she asked. "Well," John said hesitantly, "because all birds return to the earth."

"Oh," said Jessie, "then we have to bury it." A box was found, the little bird was laid in the box, a paper napkin was added as a shroud, and a few minutes later a little procession was formed with Daddy, Mama, Jessie, and her little sister. Daddy carried the box, Jessie the homemade cross. After a grave was dug and the little sparrow was buried, John put a piece of moss over the grave and Jessie planted the cross upon it. Then John asked Jessie: "Do you want to say a prayer?" "Yes," replied Jessie firmly, and after having told her baby sister in no uncertain terms to fold her hands, she prayed: "Dear God, we have buried this little sparrow. Now you be good to her or I will kill you. Amen."

As they walked home John said to Jessie, "You didn't have to threaten God." Jessie answered, "I just wanted to be sure."

Well, between all the stories about the Pope, the Dalai Lama, and the other leaders of this world, Jessica's story told me most about the human heart: compassionate—but ready to kill when afraid.

The Road to Daybreak

2

A TALE OF ANCIENT INDIA

The man and woman of the nuclear age have lost naive faith in the possibilities of technology and are painfully aware that the same powers that enable them to create new lifestyles carry the potential for self-destruction.

Let me tell you an old tale of ancient India which might help us to capture the situation of humanity in the nuclear age:

Four royal sons were questioning what specialty they should master. They said to one another, "Let us search the earth and learn a special science." So they decided, and after they had agreed on a place where they would meet again, the four brothers started off, each in a different direction. Time went by, and the brothers met again at the appointed meeting place, and they asked one another what they had learned. "I have mastered a science," said the first, "which makes it possible for me, if I have nothing but a piece of bone of some creature, to create straightaway the flesh that goes with it." "I," said the second, "know how to grow that creature's skin and hair if there is flesh on its bones." The third said, "I am able to create its limbs if I have the flesh, the skin, and the hair." "And I," concluded the fourth, "know how to give life to that creature if its form is complete with limbs."

Thereupon the four brothers went into the jungle to find a piece of bone so that they could demonstrate their specialties. As fate would have it, the bone they found was a lion's, but they did not know that and picked up the bone. One added flesh to the bone, the second grew hide and hair, the third completed it with matching limbs, and the fourth gave the lion life. Shaking its heavy mane, the ferocious beast arose with its menacing mouth, sharp teeth, and merciless claws and jumped on its creators. The beast killed them all and vanished contentedly into the jungle.[1]

The man and woman of the nuclear age realize that their creative powers hold the potential for self-destruction. They see that in this nuclear age vast new industrial complexes enable people to produce in one hour that which they labored over for years in the past, but they also realize that these same industries have disturbed the ecological balance and, through air and noise pollution, have contaminated their own milieu. They drive in cars, listen to the radio, and watch TV, but have lost their ability to understand the workings of the instruments they use. They see such an abundance of material commodities around them that scarcity no longer motivates their lives, but at the same time they are groping for a direction and asking for meaning and purpose. In all this they suffer from the inevitable knowledge that their time is a time in which it has become possible for human beings to destroy not only life but also the possibility of rebirth, not only human beings but also human-kind, not only periods of existence but also history itself. For the nuclear man and woman the future has become an option.

The Wounded Healer

Apocalypse Now

Armero no longer exists. Last Wednesday night the volcano
Nevada del Ruiz in Colombia erupted and covered the town of
Armero with mud. More than twenty-one thousand people lost
their lives. When Madame Vanier first mentioned it to me,
something happened within me that I still cannot fully describe.
The total futility of existence and the incomprehensible majesty
of God touched me at the same time in the heart of my being. I
felt powerless, useless, lost in the great mass of humanity. But I
also felt a strange jealousy toward those who lay buried under
the mud together with their friends, families, doctors, and
priests, their animals and all they had. Is this blanket of mud
that snuffed out the life and the light of a whole city within a
few minutes a sign of God's wrath or of God's mercy? Do I want
to escape their fate or join them in their grave?

There is a picture in *La Croix*, the French Catholic daily,
showing the beautiful dead face of Omayra Sanchez, a twelve-
year-old girl. For sixty hours she struggled in a torrent of water
and mud. The rescue team could not free her pinned legs. She
died with a cry of hope and love. Her peaceful face, surrounded
by the debris and destruction, speaks of something beyond the
despair of human life. Her whole being seems to cry out: "Love,
love, love one another and no power will be able to overcome
you." Her death explains something of my own feeling, which
reaches beyond feelings. I am neither angry nor glad, neither
sad nor happy. I am filled neither with grief nor consolation.
What I experience after learning about the sudden death of
more than twenty thousand people cannot be grasped by any

emotion. I keep looking at Omayra's face and hear deep within me a voice saying: "Know that you are loved and called to love. Love now and do not fear . . . all is well." As I pray and lift the thousands of people buried in Armero up to God, I see once again Rembrandt's painting of the old father welcoming his lost son home. His large red cape has become so wide that it covers the whole globe. He says again: "You are safe, my children, you are safe with me. I love you all with a love that never dies. Do not be afraid, but love one another as I love you."

Ronald Reagan and Mikhail Gorbachev, the two most powerful men in this world, are speaking with each other in Geneva today. Will they be able to bring peace to our war-torn world, or is their meeting a somber prelude to a nuclear holocaust? I wish they could both listen to Omayra's last cry of hope and love, look together at her dead face, forgive each other in the name of their countries, and promise each other to let love overcome their fears.

Unpublished journal

Mysticism in a Nuclear Age

It is my growing conviction that in Jesus the mystical and the revolutionary ways are not opposites, but two sides of the same human mode of experiential transcendence. I am increasingly convinced that conversion is the individual equivalent of revolution. Therefore, every real revolutionary is challenged to be a mystic at heart, and one who walks the mystical way is called to unmask the illusory quality of human society. Mysticism and revolution are two aspects of the same attempt to bring about radical change. No mystics can prevent themselves from becoming social critics, since in self-reflection they will discover the roots of a sick society. Similarly, no revolutionaries can avoid facing their own human condition, since in the midst of their struggle for a new world they will find that they are also fighting their own reactionary fears and false ambitions.

Mystics, and revolutionaries as well, must cut loose from their selfish needs for a safe and protected existence and face without fear their own miserable condition and that of the world around them. . . .

For a Christian, Jesus is the one in whom it has indeed become manifest that revolution and conversion cannot be separated in the human search for experiential transcendence. The appearance of Jesus in our midst has made it undeniably clear that changing the human heart and changing human society are not separate tasks, but are as interconnected as the two beams of the cross.

Jesus was a revolutionary who did not become an extremist since he did not offer an ideology, but himself. He was also a mystic who did not use his intimate relationship with God to avoid the social evils of his time, but shocked his milieu to the point of being executed as a rebel. In this sense he also remains for men and women of the nuclear age the way to liberation and freedom.

The Wounded Healer

Thomas Merton on Gandhi and Nonviolence

1

One of the deepest of Merton's insights which he formulated in the book *Gandhi on Nonviolence* is that the spirit of truth is the spirit of nonviolence. The spirit of truth reveals to us that our present situation is not definitive but rather carries within itself the possibility of conversion to the good. Merton wrote:

> Hence nonviolence implies a kind of bravery far different from violence. In the use of force, one simplifies the situation by assuming that the evil to be overcome is clear-cut, definite, and irreversible. Hence there remains but one thing: to eliminate it. Any dialogue with the sinner, any question of the irreversibility of his act, only means faltering and failure. Failure to eliminate evil is itself a defeat. . . . The greatest of tyrannies are all therefore based on the postulate that *there should never be any sin.*

> (*Gandhi on Nonviolence*)

Here Merton touched the core of nonviolence. Nonviolence stands or falls according to the vision of evil. If evil is seen only as an irreversible, clearly visible, and sharply outlined tumor, then there is only one possibility: cut it out. And then violence is necessary. But when evil is reversible and can be turned into good through forgiveness, then nonviolence is a possibility. Since Merton had experienced in his own life that forgiveness is possible through Christ, nonviolence became then not only a possibility, but even a prerequisite for being Christian.

Thomas Merton: Contemplative Critic

2

In a very impressive way, Merton showed how this nonviolence can give form to a new community. He said:

> A violent change would not have been a serious change at all. To punish and destroy the oppressor is merely to initiate a new cycle of violence and oppression. The only real liberation is that which *liberates both the oppressor and the oppressed* at the same time from the same tyrannical automatism of the violent process which contains in itself the curse of irreversibility. . . .
>
> True freedom is then inseparable from the inner strength which can assume the common burden of evil which weighs both on oneself and one's adversary. False freedom is only a manifestation of the weakness that cannot bear even one's evil until it is projected on the other and seen as exclusively his. The highest form of spiritual freedom is, as Gandhi believed, to be sought in the strength of heart which is capable of liberating the oppressed and the oppressor together. But in any event, the oppressed must be able to be free within himself, so that he may begin to gain strength to pity his oppressor. . . .
>
> *(Gandhi on Nonviolence)*

Here we have come back to the compassion that must be formed in one's heart, a compassion that comes out of a deep experience of solidarity, in which one recognizes that the evil, sin, and violence which one sees in the world and in the other are deeply rooted in one's own heart. Only when you want to confess this and want to rely on the merciful God who can bring good out of evil are you in a position to receive forgiveness and also to give it to other men and women who threaten you with violence. Precisely because Merton had discovered this nonviolent compassion in his solitude could he in a real sense be a monk, that is to say, one who unmasks through his criticism the illusions of a violent society and who wants to change the world in spirit and truth.

Thomas Merton: Contemplative Critic

Ecstasy in
a Nuclear Age

I consider it very important to reclaim the word *ecstasy* for all Christian people who strive to move from the house of fear to the house of love. . . .

Ecstasy comes from the Greek *ekstasis*, which in turn is derived from *ek*, meaning "out," and *stasis*, a state of standstill. To be ecstatic literally means to be outside of a static place. Thus, those who live ecstatic lives are always moving away from rigidly fixed situations and exploring new, unmapped dimensions of reality. . . .

Ecstasy is always a movement toward a shared life. Static living separates us and turns us into isolated individuals fighting for our own individual survival. But ecstatic living leads us to the place where new life is discovered "among" us. It makes us break through our walls of isolation and become a people of God, people who proclaim the joy of the eternal life that has already begun. It is the first sign of the kingdom that Jesus came to proclaim. . . .

Ecstatic living entails a constant willingness to leave the safe, secure, familiar place and to reach out to others, even when that involves risking one's own security. On an international scale this means a foreign policy that goes far beyond the question "How can our nation survive?" It would be a policy primarily concerned with the survival of humanity and willing to make national sacrifices. It would be a policy which realizes that idolizing the security of the nation endangers the whole of humanity. It would be a policy which places being human before being American, Russian, Cuban, Nicaraguan, or Mexican. In short, it would be a policy that seeks to liberate nations from their mutual fear and offers ways to celebrate our common humanity.

Ecstasy always reaches out to new freedom. As long as national security is our primary concern and national survival more important than preserving life on this planet, we continue to live in the house of fear. Ultimately, we must choose between security—individual, social, or national—and freedom.

Freedom is the true human goal. Life is true only if it is free. An obsessive concern for security freezes us; it leads us to rigidity, fixation, and eventually death. The more preoccupied we are with security the more visible the force of death becomes, whether in the form of a pistol beside our bed, a rifle in our house, or a Trident submarine in our port.

Lifesigns

A Parable

I wrote the following parable to illustrate the disastrous results of an obsessive preoccupation with national security:

Once there was a people who surveyed the resources of the world and said to each other: "How can we be sure that we will have enough in hard times? We want to survive whatever happens. Let us start collecting food, materials, and knowledge so that we are safe and secure when a crisis occurs." So they started hoarding, so much and so eagerly that other peoples protested and said: "You have much more than you need, while we don't have enough to survive. Give us part of your wealth!" But the fearful hoarders said: "No, no, we need to keep this in case of an emergency, in case things go bad for us, too, in case our lives are threatened." But the others said: "We are dying *now*, please give us food and materials and knowledge to survive. We can't wait . . . we need it now!" Then the fearful hoarders became ever more fearful since they became afraid that the poor and hungry would attack them. So they said to one another: "Let us build walls around our wealth so that no stranger can take it from us." They started erecting walls so high that they could not even see anymore whether there were enemies outside the walls or not! As their fear increased they told each other: "Our enemies have become so numerous that they may be able to tear down our walls. Our walls are not strong enough to keep them away. We need to put bombs on top of the walls so that nobody will dare to even come close to us." But instead of feeling safe and secure behind their armed walls they found themselves trapped in the prison they had built with their own fear. They even became afraid of their own bombs, wondering if they might harm themselves more than their enemy. And gradually they realized their fear of death had brought them closer to it.

While the instruments of death escalate in number, complexity, and scope, enabling us to destroy the human race within a few days, we continue to be preoccupied with defending national boundaries, national pride, and national honor. We forget that the ways we have chosen to defend ourselves endanger us as much as our enemies. Never have nations spent so much to protect themselves against their neighbors near and far, and never have we come so close to the annihilation of the human race.

There is an urgent need for a spirituality that addresses these idolatries and opens the way to a new ecstasy. We must find a way to go beyond our national security obsession and reach out and foster life for all people, whatever their nationality, race, or religion.

Lifesigns

The Task
of Peacemaking

NUCLEAR AGE—A NEW SEASON

Every one of the eight beatitudes that Jesus proclaimed in the Sermon on the Mount are for all people and for all times. But there are times in which one word speaks louder than another. In the thirteenth century St. Francis brought to the foreground the blessing on the poor. In the nineteenth century many saints and visionaries called new attention to the blessing on the pure of heart. Clearly our century is the century of the peacemakers. Qoheleth says: "There is a season for everything, a time . . . for keeping silent, a time for speaking . . . a time for war, a time for peace" (Ecc. 3:7–8). If this century will be remembered, it will be remembered for those who gave themselves for the cause of peace.

Peacework (unpublished)

A HAUNTING QUESTION
FROM THE PAST

When the Second World War came to an end, I was only thirteen years old. Although my parents had protected me and my brother quite skillfully from the horror of the Nazis, they couldn't prevent me from seeing how our Jewish neighbors were led away and from hearing about concentration camps to which they were deported and from which they never returned. Only in the years after the war did I become aware of the demonic dimensions of the Jewish persecution and learn the word *holocaust*. And now, forty years later, I often ask myself: "Why was there not a massive popular uprising? Why weren't there marches of thousands of people protesting the genocide that was taking place? Why did the millions of religious people not invade the camps and tear down the gas chambers and ovens that were being built to annihilate the Jewish people? Why did those who prayed, sang hymns, and went to church not resist the powers of evil so visible in their own land?"

It is important to find answers for these questions. But today I am no longer a thirteen-year-old boy who does not fully understand what is going on.

Today I am an adult living only a few miles from the place where the Trident submarine is being built, a weapon able to destroy in one second more people than were gassed in Nazi Germany during the long years of the Hitler regime. Today I am a well-informed person fully aware of the genocide in Guatemala and the murderous terror in El Salvador. Today I am a well-educated teacher who is able to show clearly and convincingly that the costly arms race between the superpowers means starvation for millions of people all over the globe. Today I am a Christian who has heard the words of Christ many times and knows that the God of Israel and the God of Jesus Christ is the God of the living in whom there is no shadow of death. Today I am asking myself the question: "Does my prayer, my communion with the God of life, become visible in acts of resistance against the powers of death surrounding me?" Or will those who are thirteen years old today raise the same question forty years from now that I am raising about the adult Christians of my youth? I have to realize that my silence or apathy may make it impossible for anyone to raise any

questions forty years from today. Because what is being prepared is not a holocaust to extinguish a whole people but a
holocaust that puts an end to humanity itself. That indeed will
not only make giving answers but also raising questions a total
impossibility.

Peacework (unpublished)

A CLEAR,
UNAMBIGUOUS "NO!"

Recently I heard the story of a twelve-year-old boy living in
New York City. He is a playful, affectionate, and very intelligent child. He has been raised with great love by his parents
and he behaves like other children of his age. But at unexpected
moments, in the middle of the night or when his mother plans
to leave the house, he suddenly screams out in fear and anguish. When his parents ask him what is happening, he clings
to them and cries: "I am afraid that the world will end."

Many children carry this fear within them and it is no secret
anymore that countless young Americans wonder if they will
ever see adulthood. Thus the nuclear threat not only can bring
untold destruction in the future, but is already destroying the
hearts and minds of many people today. It is obvious that all
people who believe that God is a God of life, and especially we
who proclaim that Jesus Christ came to live among us to
overcome the powers of death, must say "No" to nuclear arms, a
clear and unambiguous "No." The thought that human beings
are considering saving their lives by killing millions of their
fellow human beings is so preposterous that the words "saving
life" have lost all of their meaning. One of the most tragic facts
of our century is that this "No" against the nuclear arms race has
been spoken so seldom, so softly, and by so few.

Peacework (unpublished)

AN ORIGINAL SITUATION

The nuclear threat has created a situation that humanity has never faced before. History is filled with violence, cruelties, and atrocities committed by people against people. Cities, countries, and whole civilizations have been erased from this planet and millions of people have become the victims of hatred and revenge. But never before has it been possible for humanity to commit collective suicide, to destroy the whole planet, and put an end to all of history. This awesome capability was not even within our reach during the Second World War. Only its ending by the bombing of Hiroshima and Nagasaki gave us an inkling of what a next war might look like. Today, only forty-some years after these crimes against humanity, our world counts fifty thousand warheads—many of them in the megaton range—which means that they are orders of magnitude more powerful than the bombs dropped on Hiroshima and Nagasaki. A future world war cannot be compared with any previous war. It will be a war that not only ends all war but also all peace.

It is this totally "original" situation that makes a "No" to war a universal necessity. It can no longer be seen as a necessity for certain people at certain times. When the being or not-being of humanity itself is at stake, we cannot allow ourselves to be distracted by other urgencies. Because nuclear war threatens not just the lives of millions but also any future in which the dead can be remembered, this threat overarches all other threats as cause for resistance.

The small groups of "disobedient" people who here and there jump the fences of nuclear weapons facilities, climb on board nuclear submarines, or put their bodies in front of nuclear transports are trying to wake us up to a reality we continue to ignore or deny. Their small number should not mislead us. Throughout history the truth has seldom, if ever, been spoken by majorities. Statistics are not the way truth becomes known.

The prophets of Israel, Jesus and his few disciples, and the small bands of holy men and women throughout history are there to make us wonder if "these crazy peaceniks" might after all not be as important for our conversion today as St. Francis and his followers were seven centuries ago. Their loud, clear, and often dramatic "No" has to make us wonder what kind of "No" *we* are called to speak.

Peacework (unpublished)

SENTENCES ON PEACEMAKING

We cannot love issues, but we can love people, and the love of people reveals to us the way to deal with issues.

When peacemaking is based on fear it is not much different from warmaking.

Only those who deeply know that they are loved and rejoice in that love can be true peacemakers.

Prayer—living in the presence of God—is the most radical peace action we can imagine. Prayer *is* peacemaking and not simply the preparation before, the support during, and the thanksgiving after.

Prayer is not primarily a way to get something done. In prayer we undo the fear of death and therefore the basis of all human destruction.

Peacework (unpublished)

To the degree that we are dead to the world, we can live creatively in it. To the degree that we have divested ourselves of false belongings, we can live in the midst of turmoil and chaos. And to the degree that we are free of fear, we can move into the heart of danger.

Thus the act of prayer is the basis and source of all action. When our actions against the arms race are not based on the act of prayer, they easily become fearful, fanatical, bitter, and more an expression of survival instincts than of our faith in God and the God of the living.

Peacework (unpublished)

Only by belonging to Christ and Christ alone can we truly resist the devastating powers of evil and work together in this world to avoid a collective suicide. Those who do not belong to this world are the only ones who can bring it the peace it craves. Those whose lives are securely anchored beyond the powers and principalities that rule the world can enter that world freely and bring it peace.

Christ is the first peacemaker since he opened the house of God to all people and thus made the old creation new. We are sent to this world to be peacemakers in his name.

Peacework (unpublished)

Resistance

A CHILD SHALL LEAD

Having a baby seems such a natural, obvious, and rather unspectacular event. But for those who are deeply aware that we are living on a planet that is being prepared for total destruction, in a time that can be sure only of the past and the present but not of the future, and in a place that is filled with pictures of death, giving life to a new human being becomes an act of resistance. Bringing into the world a little child totally dependent on the care of others and leading it gradually to maturity is true defiance of the power of death and darkness. It is saying loudly: For us life is stronger than death, love is stronger than fear, and hope is stronger than despair.

Peacework (unpublished)

THE REAL "THREAT": PEACEMAKERS

One of the most surprising experiences in my own struggle to be a peacemaker has been the intense anger I saw in the eyes of those whose policies I questioned. For some time I believed that a good argument could convince. As I was trying to convince leaders in state and church that military intervention by the United States in Central America was immoral, illegal, and unjust, I was often met not with arguments which could disprove my point but with outright hatred as if my ideas were directly inspired by the enemy and as if listening to them would already be a lack of patriotism. The closer I came to the center of power, the more I realized how much of a threat peacemakers are to warmakers. The possibility that the warmakers' world might be built on a lie makes the peacemaker the greatest enemy of all, for peace requires us to see and accept the truth.

I have little doubt that as nonviolent peacemakers continue to do what they are now doing, they will be persecuted, mal-treated, and thrown into jail in increasing numbers. The closer we come to war, the harsher peacemakers will be treated. The greater the need for popular support of war efforts, the more ruthlessly resisters will be treated. Once I heard an American Christian say to a Korean minister: "You went to prison and suffered long for your conviction, but what can we who live such comfortable lives here in the United States do for peace?" The Korean smiled gently and said: "If you just continue to act as a Christian, you will soon be where I was!"

Peacework (unpublished)

THE CHURCH AS ENEMY

I have a great dream that one day soon Easter will become the great day of resistance, on which the resurrection of Christ is lifted up as the victory of God over all the forces of death, on which the risen Lord is proclaimed as the Lord of history, and on which all people who belong to God's kingdom, whether Russians or Americans, Cubans, Nicaraguans, Indians, or Japanese, will together protect our planet from total destruction. When that happens, churches no longer will be just places where people try to find some consolation in the midst of their daily struggles and some support in living their next week, but the center from where God's word of peace goes out over this world and to which it does not return without having borne fruit. Recently a U.S. general said at a Pentagon meeting: "Our real enemy is the Church." If all churches would reclaim the true significance of Easter as the day of the victory of life over death, all generals and armies should indeed tremble when that day approaches!

Peacework (unpublished)

RESISTING TOGETHER

If life is going to be harder for those who say "No" to war and "Yes" to life, how then can Christian resisters and nonviolent peacemakers stay alive in this world? The simple answer is: together. As long as we look at resistance as performing individual acts of heroism, there won't be many peacemakers who will survive the enormous pressures put upon them. Resistance which makes for peace is not so much the effort of brave and courageous individuals as the work of the community of faith. Individual people, even the best and the strongest, will soon be exhausted and discouraged, but a community of resistance can persevere even when its members have their moments of weakness and despair. Peacemaking can be a lasting work only when we live and work together. Community is indispensable for a faithful and enduring resistance. Without community we will be quickly sucked back into the dark world of needs and wounds, of violence and destruction, of evil and death.

Peacework (unpublished)

GRATITUDE AND PEACEMAKING

If there is any word that should characterize the life of peace-makers, it is the word *gratitude*. True peacemakers are grateful persons, persons who constantly recognize and celebrate the peace of God within and among them. This might at first sound quite romantic, but those who have lived through periods of true pain and agony know the mystery of gratitude. They have come to experience that where they meet the suffering Christ they also meet the Christ of peace. Whenever our suffering becomes Christ's suffering and our agony Christ's agony, we know in our innermost being that suffering and agony will not be able to destroy our gratitude since we have found our peace in him, a peace that is not of this world. To say thanks in the face of a nuclear holocaust threatening our planet with the extinction of all human life seems ridiculous, but when we realize that Christ also suffered this nuclear agony and anguish and overcame it on the Cross, then our gratitude can even be deeper and stronger.

Peacework (unpublished)

THE HARDEST CHALLENGE: LOVE YOUR ENEMY

One of the reasons that so many people have developed strong reservations about the peace movements is precisely that they do not see the peace they seek in the peacemakers themselves. Often what they see are fearful and angry people trying to convince others of the urgency of their protest. Thus the tragedy is that peacemakers often reveal more of the demons they are fighting than of the peace they want to bring.

The words of Jesus go right to the heart of our struggle: "Love your enemy, do good to those who hate you, bless those who curse you, pray for those who treat you badly" (Luke 6:27–28). The more I reflect on these words, the more I consider them to be the test for peacemakers.

What my enemy deserves is not my anger, rejection, resentment, or disdain, but my love. Spiritual guides throughout history have said that love for the enemy is the cornerstone of the message of Jesus and the core of holiness. For us fearful people, loving our enemy is the greatest challenge, because our fears make us divide the world between people who are for us and people who are against us, people to love and people to hate, friends and enemies.

All these distinctions are based on the illusion that others decide who we are and that our very being depends on their words, thoughts, and actions. Loving our enemy thus compels us to unmask this illusion by acting according to the knowledge that God loves all human persons regardless of their sex, religion, race, color, nationality, age, or intelligence—with the same bold, unconditional love. The distinction between friends and enemies is made by us fearful people, not by our loving God.

Therefore it is essential for peacemakers to be deeply rooted in this all-embracing love of God, who "causes the sun to rise on the bad as well as the good, and the rain to fall on honest and dishonest people alike" (Matt. 5:45). It is only this deep rootedness in God's all-inclusive love that can prevent the peacemaker from being ravaged by the same anger, resentment, and violence that lead to war.

Peacework (unpublished)

WAR AND PEACE

As a community of peacemakers it is our task first of all to recognize and affirm the great human gifts the warmakers carry within themselves. We have to see them as caring, loving, concerned human beings, who, just as we, desire peace and freedom, even though they are for fighting as the way to it.

As much as we have to confess our own dark forces to each other, so much do we have to reveal the gifts of peace in those whose lives and works we hope to change. When those who are for fighting recognize that they have real talents for peacemaking within and among them, they may become free enough to let go of their fears and claim their ability to live together as brothers and sisters without guns, bombs, B52s, cruise missiles, and Trident submarines. Many conflicts between people are rooted in their deep-seated self-loathing. This makes them think little of themselves and makes them rely more on suspicion than on trust. But to the degree that people recognize their human talents to make peace and claim them as God-given gifts, the hances for disarmament become real. In the face of the possibility of peace, war can gradually be considered a very old-fashioned way of living together.

Peacework (unpublished)

PRAYER AS RESISTANCE

Resistance can never be an anxious attempt to prevent something terrible from happening. On the contrary it is a "No" that flows forth from the true presence of the Lord, who says: "I am the Life" (John 14:6). Therefore, too, prayer can never be a panicky request to avoid a disaster. In the daily life of the community, prayer is first of all an expression of thanks for what we already have received. Even a cry for God's help cannot be separated from a spirit of gratitude. We do not ask to convince a hesitant giver.

Peacework (unpublished)

Second Coming

The coming again of Christ is his coming in judgment. The question that will sound through the heavens and the earth will be the question that we always tend to remain deaf to. Our lives as we live them seem like lives that anticipate questions that never will be asked. It seems as if we are getting ourselves ready for the question "How much did you earn during your lifetime?" or "How many friends did you make?" or "How much progress did you make in your career?" or "How much influence did you have on people?" or "How many books did you write?" or "How many conversions did you make?" Were any of these to be the question Christ will ask when he comes again in glory, many of us in North America could approach the judgment day with great confidence.

But nobody is going to hear any of these questions. The question we all are going to face is the question we are least prepared for. It is the question: "What have you done for the least of mine?"

It is the question of the just judge who in that question reveals to us that making peace and working for justice can never be separated. As long as there are people who are less than we, in whatever way or form, the question of the last judgment will be with us. As long as there are strangers; hungry, naked, and sick people; prisoners, refugees, and slaves; people who are handicapped physically, mentally, or emotionally; people without work, a home, or a piece of land, there will be that haunting question from the throne of judgment: "What have you done for the least of mine?"

This question makes the coming of Christ an ever-present event. It challenges us to look at our world agonized by wars and rumors of war and to wonder if we have not fallen into the temptation to think that peace can be separated from justice. But why would there be wars if all people had enough food, enough work, enough land? Why would there be so many guns, tanks, nuclear warheads, submarines, and other instruments of destruction if the world were not divided according to those who have the most, those who have more than enough, those who have just enough, those who have less than enough, and those who have the least?

When we look at the painful struggles of the people in South and Central America, it is not hard to realize who the least are. In most of the countries below our southern border, a very few have the most, and most have the least, and there is little in between. This state of flagrant injustice that causes the oppression and exploitation of many by a few is artificially maintained by the nations in which most people have the most and a few have the least. "Protecting our vital interests" has become the standard euphemism for maintaining the inequality among peoples and nations. It also is the main rationale for an internationally interlocking military network built on the illusion that an ever-increasing power is the only thing that keeps this world from disintegrating into chaos. Thus the world becomes an absurd world in which every year thousands of people die from hunger and violence, and in which those who cause these deaths are convinced that they do this to defend the great spiritual values of the free world.

As Jesus predicted, many will commit crimes thinking that they are doing something virtuous in the name of God. And as death and destruction increase, there are fewer people who can explain what is happening for what reason. Thus the world plunges itself deeper and deeper into absurdity—which literally means "deep deafness"—becoming less and less able to hear the question of the coming Christ: "What have you done for the least of mine?"

"Christ of the Americas," *America*, April 21, 1984

Last Judgment

1

A NEW READING

It is my impression that most people understand the question of the coming Christ as a question directed to individual people. All through Christian history there have been men and women who have listened with great attentiveness to this question and radically changed their lives in response to it. Many have dedicated their entire lives to work with the poor, the sick, and the dying. Thus we can say that the question of the day of judgment has already borne fruit.

But when we read the twenty-fifth chapter of Matthew's Gospel carefully, it becomes clear that the question of the coming of Christ is not directed to individuals alone but to nations as well. The story of the last judgment opens with the words, "When the Son of Man comes in his glory, escorted by all the angels, then he will take his seat on his throne of glory. All nations will be assembled before him" (Matt. 25:31–32). These words open a new perspective on the final question: "What have you done for the least of mine?" They make us wonder what it means that we will be judged not only as individuals but as nations as well.

Often it seems that we have heard the invitation of Jesus to be humble, compassionate, and forgiving, to take the last place, to carry our cross and lose our life as an invitation for our individual lives, our family lives, or our lives within the communities of prayer and service. . . .

But when it comes to the relationship among nations, when we are dealing with decisions that have implications for our nation's role in the world, when we are thinking about our national security and its political ramifications, then we suddenly reverse our attitude completely and consider the Gospel demands as utterly naive. When it comes to politics, power is the issue, and those who suggest that the powerless way of Christ is also the way to which the nations are called find themselves quickly accused as betrayers of their country. As nations—so we hear—we cannot seriously listen to the question "What have you done for the least of mine?" Looking at small nations struggling to overcome their hunger, thirst, estrangement, nakedness, and imprisonment as the least of our brothers and sisters would require a radical change in the use of power, a change from using power to dominate to using power to serve. Many would consider such a change political suicide.

"Christ of the Americas," *America*, April 21, 1984

2

LAST JUDGMENT: WHO WILL BE THE JUDGE?

The Apostle Paul writes: "In your minds you must be as Christ Jesus. His state was divine, yet he did not cling to his equality with God but emptied himself to assume the condition of a slave and become as we are" (Phil. 2:5, 7). Are these words also words for the nations? Is it possible that a nation can become one among the nations as Christ became one among us? If it is true that the question of the returning Christ is also a question for the nations, then that question requires not only an individual but also a national conversion. As long as the overarching goal of the United States is to be at all costs the most powerful nation of the earth, we may become the reluctant participants in the hastening of the judgment day, since in this nuclear age the cost for remaining the most powerful nation on the earth quite likely is the end of all human life on this planet.

Thus we are faced with the greatest spiritual challenge ever presented: to be converted as a nation and follow the humble way of Christ. Is that a possibility? It has become a necessity for our survival. It has become our most urgent task to find our true identity among the nations and to let go of the illusory identities that continue to breed one war after another. The tragedy is that the political discussion among our people and their representatives has been narrowed down so much that no truly political concern can be brought to the foreground without threatening the political survival. When the main question has become "Should the Sandinista regime be overthrown overtly or covertly?" politics has already become the victim of the totalitarianism it is trying to stop from coming close to its borders.

The real issue that faces us today is: "What does it mean to be a nation in a world that is able to destroy itself at any moment?" That is the issue that has to be brought to the center of the attention of our people. If ever, it is today that politicians are called to be wise people, that is, women and men who can raise the issue of national identity and offer a vision of how to be a nation living in harmony among nations freely using its power to serve rather than dominate. I sense that many personal sacrifices in the political arena will be necessary to reach the point of national discussion aiming at national conversion. Many who possess political power today will need to risk their own political futures and will have to be willing to let go of oppressive power in order to empower other nations and thus further justice and peace in the world. Without such sacrifices there will no longer be a true dialogue in the world of politics, but only a tyrannical monologue leading to the absurd silence not only of politicians but of all human beings. Then we will have created our own day of judgment and will have become our own judges.

This is precisely what the last judgment is all about. The Lord who becomes one of us in humility does not really judge us but reveals to us what we have become to one another. The day of judgment is in fact the day of recognition, the day on which we see for ourselves what we have done to our brothers and sisters, and how we have treated the divine body of which we are part.

Thus the question "What have you done for the least of mine?" is not only the question of injustice and the question of peace, it also is the question by which we judge ourselves. The answer to that question will determine the existence or nonexistence of our human family.

"Christ of the Americas," *America*, April 21, 1984

FINAL MOVEMENT: THE BEETHOVEN FACTOR

The Fifth Symphony of Beethoven now sounds as if it always existed. We find it so familiar that we can hardly believe there was once a time without it, and that each movement had to be conceived note by note by a human being. It was not written in the stars, it had to be made.

So, too, new ways must be found for nations to lift up their unity in global celebration, and praise the Creator in ecstatic, joyful song. Most people despair that such a peace is possible. They cling to old ways and prefer the security offered by preparing for war to the insecurity of taking risks for peace. But the few who dare to sing a new song of peace are the new St. Francises of our time. They offer a glimpse of a new order that is being born out of the ruin of the old. The world is waiting for new saints, ecstatic men and women who are so deeply rooted in the love of God that they are free to envision a new international order—where justice reigns and war is no longer the preferred way to solve conflicts among nations.

Lifesigns

Prayer for a Nuclear Age

Dear Lord, awaken the people of the earth and their leaders to the realization of the madness of the nuclear arms race. Today we mourn the dead of past wars, but will there be anyone to mourn the dead of the next one? O Lord, turn us away from our foolish race to self-destruction; let us see that more and more weaponry indeed means more of a chance to use it. Please, Lord, let the great talents you have given to your creatures not fall into the hands of the powers and principalities for whom death is the means as well as the goal. Let us see that the resources hidden in your earth are for feeding each other, healing each other, offering shelter to each other, making this world a place where men, women, and children of all races and nations can live together in peace.

Give us new prophets who can speak openly, directly, convincingly, and lovingly to kings, presidents, senators, church leaders, and all men and women of good will, prophets who can make us wage peace instead of war. Lord, make haste to help us. Do not come too late! Amen.

A Cry for Mercy

NOTES:

[1] *Tales of Ancient India*, translated from the Sanskrit by J.A.B. van Buitenen, New York: Bantam Books, 1961, pp. 50–51.

EPILOGUE

Adam's Story:
The Peace That Is Not
of This World

LECTURE GIVEN AT HARVARD
ST. PAUL'S CATHOLIC CHURCH, CAMBRIDGE
FEBRUARY 10, 1987

Text published in *Weavings*,
March–April 1988

INTRODUCTION

How to speak about peace? During the past years my own life
has gone through so many changes that I have lost much of my
self-confidence. A few years ago it seemed rather easy to get up
in front of many people and give some suggestions about how
to be people of peace. I was able to do that with a certain ease
and with the conviction that I had something important to say.

As I was preparing this presentation, however, I experienced a
deep inner emptiness, a sense of futility in regard to words,
even a despair about saying anything about peace, peacemaking, or a spirituality of peace. I was tempted to call it off. My
poverty seemed too paralyzing.

But I am here and the reason is that I finally decided to share
my poverty and trust that God does not want me to hide it
from you. In the past I have often said that prayer, resistance,
and community are the three core aspects of peace work. I still

believe that this is true, but I question the value of saying it. Do these concepts generate what they express? I am no longer as sure as I was before. I am no longer sure of the use of any words in helping us to become the people God calls us to be.

So what to do now? After some agonizing hours of thinking about it all, I felt that I should tell you a little bit about my present life and try to discover there some aspect of the peace of Jesus we are searching for.

During the past two years I moved from Harvard to Daybreak, that is from an institution for the best and the brightest to a community for mentally handicapped people. Daybreak, close to Toronto, is part of an international federation of communities called l'Arche—the Ark—where mentally handicapped men and women and their assistants try to live together in the spirit of the Beatitudes. I live in a house with six handicapped people and four assistants. None of the assistants is specially trained to work with people with a mental handicap, but we receive all the help we need from doctors, psychiatrists, behavioral management people, social workers, and physiotherapists in town. When there are no special crises, we live together as a family, gradually forgetting who is handicapped and who is not. We are simply John, Bill, Trevor, Raymond, Adam, Rose, Steve, Jane, Naomi, and Henri. We all have our gifts, our struggles, our strengths and weaknesses. We eat together, play together, pray together, and go out together. We all have our own preferences in terms of work, food, and movies, and we all have our problems in getting along with someone in the house, whether handicapped or not. We laugh a lot. We cry a lot too. Sometimes both at the same time. Every morning when I say, "Good morning, Raymond," he says, "I am not awake yet. Saying good morning to everyone each day is unreal." Christmas Eve Trevor wrapped marshmallows in silver paper as peace gifts for everyone and at the Christmas dinner he climbed on a chair, lifted his glass, and said, "Ladies and gentlemen, this is not a celebration, this is Christmas." When one of the men speaking on the phone with someone was bothered by the cigarette smoke of an assistant, he yelled angrily, "Stop smoking; I can't hear." And every guest who comes for dinner is received by Bill with the question, "Hey, tell me, what is a turkey in suspense?" When the newcomer confesses ignorance, Bill, with a big grin on his face, says, "I will tell you tomorrow." And then he starts laughing so loudly that the visitor has to laugh with him whether he finds the joke funny or not so funny.

That is l'Arche; that is Daybreak; that is the family of ten I am living with day in and day out. What can life in this family of a few poor people reveal about the peace of Christ for which we are searching? Let me tell you the story of Adam, one of the ten people in our home, and let him become the silent spokesman of the peace that is not of this world.

Never having worked with handicapped people, I was not only apprehensive, but even afraid to enter this unfamiliar world. This fear did not lessen when I was invited to work directly with Adam. Adam is the weakest person of our family. He is a twenty-five-year-old man who cannot speak, cannot dress or undress himself, cannot walk alone or eat without much help. He does not cry, or laugh, and only occasionally makes eye contact. His back is distorted and his arm and leg movements are very twisted. He suffers from severe epilepsy and, notwithstanding heavy medication, there are few days without grand mal seizures. Sometimes, as he grows suddenly rigid, he utters a howling groan, and on a few occasions I have seen a big tear coming down his cheek. It takes me about an hour and a half to wake Adam up, give him his medication, undress him, carry him into his bath, wash him, shave him, clean his teeth, dress him, walk him to the kitchen, give him his breakfast, put him in his wheelchair, and bring him to the place where he spends most of the day with different therapeutic exercises.

When a grand mal seizure occurs during this sequence of activities, much more time is needed, and often he has to return to sleep to regain some of the energy spent during such a seizure.

I tell you all of this not to give you a nursing report but to share with you something quite intimate. After a month of working this way with Adam, something started to happen to me that never had happened to me before. This deeply handicapped young man, who by many outsiders is considered an embarrassment, a distortion of humanity, a useless creature who should not have been allowed to be born, started to become my dearest companion. As my fears gradually decreased, a love started to emerge in me so full of tenderness and affection that most of my other tasks seemed boring and superficial compared with the hours spent with Adam. Out of this broken body and broken mind emerged a most beautiful human being offering me a greater gift than I would ever be able to offer him. It is hard for me to find adequate words for this experience, but somehow Adam revealed to me who he was and who I was and how we can love each other. As I carried his naked body into the bathwater, made big waves to let the water run fast around his chest and neck, rubbed noses with him and told him all sorts of stories about him and me, I knew that two friends were communicating far beyond the realm of thought or emotion. Deep speaks to deep, spirit speaks to spirit, heart speaks to heart. I started to realize that there was a mutuality of love not based on shared knowledge or shared feelings, but on shared humanity. The longer I stayed with Adam the more clearly I started to see him as my gentle teacher, teaching me what no book, school, or professor could have ever taught me.

Am I romanticizing, making something beautiful out of something ugly, projecting my hidden need to be a father on this deeply retarded man, spiritualizing what in essence is a shameful human condition that needs to be prevented at all cost? I am enough of a psychologically trained intellectual to raise these questions. Recently—during the writing of this story—Adam's parents came for a visit. I asked them: "Tell me, during all the years you had Adam in your home, what did he give you?" His father smiled and said without a moment of hesitation: "He brought us peace . . . he is our peacemaker . . . our son of peace."

Let me, then, tell you about Adam's peace, a peace which the world cannot give. I am moved by the simple fact that probably the most important task I have is to give words to the peace of one who has no words. The gift of peace hidden in Adam's utter weakness is a gift not *of* the world, but certainly *for* the world. For this gift to become known, someone has to lift it up and hand it on. That, maybe, is the deepest meaning of being an assistant to handicapped people. It is helping them to share their gifts.

1

Adam's peace is first of all a peace rooted in *being*. How simple a truth, but how hard to live! Being is more important than doing. Adam can do nothing. He is completely dependent on others every moment of his life. His gift is his pure *being with us*. Every time in the evening when I run home to "do" Adam—that means help him with his supper and put him to bed—I realize that the best thing I can do for Adam is to be with him. If Adam wants anything, it is that you be with him. And indeed that is the great joy: paying total attention to his breathing, his eating, his careful steps, looking at how he tries to lift a spoon to his mouth, or offers his left arm a little to make it easier for you to take off his shirt; always wondering about possible pains that he cannot express, but that still ask for relief.

Most of my past life has been built around the idea that my value depends on what I do. I made it through grade school, high school, and university. I earned my degrees and awards and I made my career. Yes, with many others I fought my way up to the lonely top of a little success, a little popularity, and a little power. But as I sit beside the slow and heavily breathing Adam, I start seeing how violent that journey was. So filled with desires to be better than others, so marked by rivalry and competition, so pervaded with compulsions and obsessions, and so spotted with moments of suspicion, jealousy, resentment, and revenge. Oh, sure, most of what I did was called ministry, the ministry of justice and peace, the ministry of forgiveness and reconciliation, the ministry of healing and wholeness. But when those who want peace are as interested in success, popularity, and power as those who want war, what then *is* the real difference between war and peace? When the peace is as much of this world as the war, what other choice is there but the choice between a war which we euphemistically call pacification and a peace in which the peacemakers violate one another's deepest values?

Adam says to me, "Peace is first of all the art of being." I know he is right because after four months of being with Adam I am discovering in myself a beginning of an inner at-homeness that I didn't know before. I even feel the unusual desire to do a lot less and be a lot more, preferably with Adam.

As I cover him with his sheets and blankets and turn out the lights, I pray with Adam. He is always very quiet as if he knows that my praying voice sounds a little different from my speaking voice. I whisper in his ear: "May all the angels protect you," and often he looks up at me from his pillow and seems to know what I am talking about. Since I began to pray with Adam I have come to know better than before that praying is being with Jesus and simply wasting time with Him. Adam keeps teaching me that.

2

Adam's peace is not only a peace rooted in being, but also a peace rooted in the heart. That true peace belongs to the heart is such a radical statement that only people as handicapped as Adam seem to be able to get it across! Somehow during the centuries we have come to believe that what makes us human is our minds. Many people who do not know any Latin still seem to know the definition of a human being as a reasoning animal: *rationale animal est homo* (Seneca). But Adam keeps telling me over and over again that what makes us human is not our minds but our hearts, not our ability to think but our ability to love. Whoever speaks about Adam as an animal-like creature misses the sacred mystery that Adam is fully capable of receiving and giving love. He is fully human, not a little bit human, not half human, not nearly human, but fully, completely human because he is all heart. And it is our heart that is made in the image and likeness of God. If this were not the case, how could I ever say to you that Adam and I love each other? How could I ever experience new life from simply being with him? How could I ever believe that moving away from teaching many men and women to being taught by Adam is a real step forward? I am speaking here about something very, very real. It is the primacy of the heart.

Let me say here that by heart I do not mean the seat of human emotions in contrast to the mind as the seat of human thought. No, by heart I mean the center of our being where God has hidden the divine gifts of trust, hope, and love. The mind tries to understand, grasp problems, discern different aspects of reality, and probe the mysteries of life. The heart allows us to enter into relationships and become sons and daughters of God and brothers and sisters of each other. Long before our mind is able to exercise its power, our heart is already able to develop a trusting human relationship. I am convinced that this trusting human relationship even precedes the moment of our birth.

Here we are touching the origin of the spiritual life. Often people think that the spiritual life is the latest in coming and follows the development of the biological, emotional, and intellectual life. But living with Adam and reflecting on my experience with him makes me realize that God's loving spirit has touched us long before we can walk, feel, or talk. The spiritual life is given to us from the moment of our conception. It is the divine gift of love that makes the human person able to reveal a presence much greater than himself or herself. When I say that I believe deeply that Adam can give and receive love and that there is a true mutuality between us, I do not make a naive psychological statement overlooking his severe handicaps. I am speaking about a love between us that transcends all thoughts and feelings precisely because it is rooted in God's first love, a love that precedes all human loves. The mystery of Adam is that in his deep mental and emotional brokenness he has become so empty of all human pride that he has become the preferable mediator of that first love. Maybe this will help you see why Adam is giving me a whole new understanding of God's love for the poor and the oppressed. He has offered me a new perspective on the well-known "preferential option" for the poor.

The peace that flows from Adam's broken heart is not of this world. It is not the result of political analysis, round table debates, discernment of the signs of the times, or well-thought-out strategies. All these activities of the mind have their role to play in the complex process of peacemaking. But they all will become easily perverted to a new way of warmaking if they are not put into the service of the divine peace that flows from the broken heart of those who are called the poor in spirit.

3

The third and most tangible quality of Adam's peace is that while rooted more in being than in doing and more in the heart than in the mind, it is a peace that always calls forth community. The most impressive aspect of my life at l'Arche is that the handicapped people hold us together as a family and that the most handicapped people are the true center of gravity of our togetherness. Adam in his total vulnerability calls us together as a family. And in fact, from the perspective of community formation, he turns everything upside down. The weakest members are the assistants. We come from different countries—Brazil, the United States, Canada, and Holland—and our commitments are ambiguous at best. Some stay longer than others, but most move on after one or two years. Closer to the center are Raymond, Bill, John, and Trevor, who are relatively independent but still need much help and attention. They are permanent members of the family. They are with us for life and they keep us honest. Because of them conflicts never last very long, tensions are talked out, and disagreements resolved. But in the heart of our community are Rose and Adam, both deeply handicapped, and the weaker of the two is Adam.

Adam is the most broken of us all, but without any doubt the strongest bond among us all. Because of Adam there is always someone home, because of Adam there is a quiet rhythm in the house, because of Adam there are moments of silence and quiet, because of Adam there are always words of affection, gentleness, and tenderness, because of Adam there is patience and endurance, because of Adam there are smiles and tears visible to all, because of Adam there is always space for mutual forgiveness and healing . . . yes, because of Adam there is peace among us. How otherwise could people from such different nationalities and cultures, people with such different characters and with such an odd variety of handicaps, whether mental or not, live together in peace? Adam truly calls us together around him and molds this motley group of strangers into a family. Adam, the weakest among us, is our true peacemaker. How mysterious are God's ways: "God chose those who by human standards are fools to shame the wise; he chose those who by human standards are weak to shame the strong, those who by human standards are common and contemptible—indeed who count for nothing—to reduce to nothing all those who do count for something, so that no human being might feel boastful before God" (1 Cor. 1:27–30 *author paraphrase*). Adam gives flesh to these words of Paul. He teaches me the true mystery of community.

Most of my adult life I have tried to show the world that I could do it on my own, that I needed others only to get me back on my lonely road. Those who have helped me helped me to become a strong, independent, self-motivated, creative man who would be able to survive in the long search for individual freedom. With many others, I wanted to become a self-sufficient star. And most of my fellow intellectuals joined me in that desire. But all of us highly trained individuals are facing today a world on the brink of total destruction. And now we start to wonder how we might join forces to make peace! What kind of peace can this possibly be? Who can paint a portrait of people who all want to take the center seat? Who can build a beautiful church with people who are only interested in erecting the tower? Who can bake a birthday cake with people who only want to put the candles on? You all know the problem. When all want the honor of being the final peacemaker, there never will be peace.

Adam needs many people and nobody can boast of anything. Adam will never be better. His constant seizures even make it likely that medically things will only get worse. There are no successes to claim and everyone who works with him does only a little bit. My part in his life is very, very small. Some cook for him, others do his laundry, some give him massages, others play him music, take him for a walk, a swim, or a ride. Some look after his blood pressure and regulate his medicine, others look after his teeth. But though with all this assistance Adam doesn't change and often seems to slip away in a state of total exhaustion, a community of peace has emerged around him. It is a community that certainly does not want to put its light under a basket, because the peace community that Adam has called forth is not there just for Adam, but for all who belong to Adam's race. It is a community that proclaims that God has chosen to descend among us in complete weakness and vulnerability and thus to reveal to us the glory of God.

Thus, as you see, Adam is gradually teaching me something about the peace that is not of this world. It is a peace not constructed by tough competition, hard thinking, and individual stardom, but rooted in simply being present to each other, a peace that speaks about the first love of God by which we are all held and a peace that keeps calling us to community, a fellowship of the weak. Adam has never said a word to me. He will never do so. But every night as I put him to bed I say "thank you" to him. How much closer can one come to the Word that became flesh and dwells among us?

I have told you about Adam and about Adam's peace. But you are not part of l'Arche, you do not live at Daybreak, you are not a member of Adam's family. Like me, however, you search for peace and want to find peace in your heart, your family, and your world. But looking around us in the world, we see concentration camps and refugee camps; we see overcrowded prisons; we see the burning of villages, genocidal actions, kidnappings, torture, and murder; we see starving children, neglected elderly, and countless men and women without food, shelter, or a job. We see people sleeping in the city streets, young boys and girls selling themselves for others' pleasure; we see violence and rape and the desperation of millions of fearful and lonely people. Seeing all this, we realize that there is no peace in our world. And still . . . that is what our hearts desire most. You and I may have tried giving money, demonstrating, overseas projects, and many other things—but as we grow older we are faced with the fact that the peace we waited for still has not come. Something in us is in danger of growing cold, bitter, and resentful, and we are tempted to withdraw from it all and limit ourselves to the easier task of personal survival. But that is a demonic temptation.

I have told you about Adam and his peace to offer you a quiet guide with a gentle heart who gives you a little light to walk with through this dark world. Adam does not solve anything. Even with all the support he receives, he cannot change his own utter poverty. As he grows older, he grows poorer and poorer and poorer. A little infection, an unhappy fall, an accidental swallowing of his own tongue during a seizure, and many other small incidents may take him suddenly away from us. When he dies, nobody will be able to boast about anything. And still, what a light he brings! In Adam's name I therefore say to you: "Do not give up working for peace. But always remember that the peace for which you work is not of this world. Do not let yourself be distracted by the great noises of war, the dramatic descriptions of misery, and the sensational expressions of human cruelty. The newspapers, movies, and war novels may make you numb, but they do not create in you a true desire for peace. They tend to create feelings of shame, guilt, and powerlessness and these feelings are the worst motives for peace work."

Keep your eyes on the prince of peace, the one who doesn't cling to his divine power; the one who refuses to turn stones into bread, jump from great heights, and rule with great power; the one who says, "Blessed are the poor, the gentle, those who mourn, and those who hunger and thirst for righteousness; blessed are the merciful, the pure in heart, the peacemakers and those who are persecuted in the cause of uprightness" (see Matt. 5:3–11); the one who touches the lame, the crippled, and the blind; the one who speaks words of forgiveness and encouragement; the one who dies alone, rejected and despised. Keep your eyes on him who becomes poor with the poor, weak with the weak, and who is rejected with the rejected. He is the source of all peace.

Where is this peace to be found? The answer is clear. In weakness. First of all, in our own weakness, in those places of our hearts where we feel most broken, most insecure, most in agony, most afraid. Why there? Because there our familiar ways of controlling our world are being stripped away; there we are called to let go from doing much, thinking much, and relying on our self-sufficiency. Right there where we are weakest the peace which is not of this world is hidden.

In Adam's name I say to you, "Claim that peace that remains unknown to so many and make it your own. Because with that peace in your heart you will have new eyes to see and new ears to hear and gradually recognize that same peace in places you would have least expected." Not long ago I was in Honduras. It was my first time in Central America since I had come to Daybreak and become friends with Adam. I suddenly realized that I was a little less consumed by anger about the political manipulations, a little less distracted by the blatant injustices, and a little less paralyzed by the realization that the future of Honduras looks very dark. Visiting the severely handicapped Raphael in the l'Arche community near Tegucigalpa, I saw the same peace I had seen in Adam, and hearing many stories about the gifts of joy offered by the poorest of the poor to the oh-so-serious assistants who came from France, Belgium, the United States, and Canada, I knew that peace is the gift of God often hidden from the wise and wealthy and revealed to the inarticulate and poor.

I am not saying that the questions about peace in Central America, peace in Afghanistan, peace in Northern Ireland, South Africa, Iran, and Iraq are no longer important. Far from that. I am only saying that the seeds of national and international peace are already sown on the soil of our own suffering and the suffering of the poor, and that we truly can trust that these seeds, like the mustard seeds of the Gospel, will produce large shrubs in which many birds can find a place to rest. As long as we think and live as if there is no peace yet and that it all is going to depend on ourselves to make it come about, we are on the road to self-destruction. But when we trust that the God of love has already given the peace we are searching for, we will see this peace breaking through the broken soil of our human condition and we will be able to let it grow fast and even heal the economic and political maladies of our time. With this trust in our hearts, we will be able to hear the words: "Blessed are the peacemakers, for they shall inherit the earth." It fills me with a special joy that all the Adams of this world will be the first to receive this inheritance.

CONCLUSION

It is time to end. Somehow it feels hard to end. There are so many unspoken words, unexpressed feelings, and unrevealed mysteries. But I have to trust that you will know about them even when they have remained hidden. . . .

Many people live in the night; a few live in the day. We all know about night and day, darkness and light. We know about it in our hearts; we know about it in our families and communities; we know about it in our world. The peace that the world does not give is the light that dispels the darkness. Every bit of that peace makes the day come!

Let me conclude with an old Hasidic tale that summarizes much of what I have tried to say.

> The rabbi asks his students: "How can we determine the hour of dawn, when the night ends and the day begins?"
>
> One of his students suggested: "When from a distance you can distinguish between a dog and a sheep?"

"No," was the answer of the rabbi.

"Is it when one can distinguish between a fig tree and a grapevine?" asked a second student.

"No," the rabbi said.

"Please tell us the answer, then," said the students.

"It is, then," said the wise teacher, "when you can look into the face of human beings and you have enough light [in you] to recognize them as your brothers and sisters. Up until then it is night, and darkness is still with us."

Let us pray for the light. It is the peace the world cannot give.

Bibliography

BOOKS

Intimacy: Essays in Pastoral Psychology, Fides, 1969; New York: Harper & Row, 1981.

Creative Ministry: Beyond Professionalism in Teaching, Preaching, Counseling, Organizing, and Celebrating, Garden City, New York: Doubleday, 1971.

With Open Hands, Notre Dame, Indiana: Ave Maria, 1972.

Thomas Merton: Contemplative Critic (originally titled *Pray to Live*), Fides, 1972; New York: Harper & Row, 1981.

The Wounded Healer: Ministry in Contemporary Society, Garden City, New York: Doubleday, 1972.

Aging: The Fulfillment of Life, co-authored with Walter Gaffney, Garden City, New York: Doubleday, 1974.

Out of Solitude: Three Meditations on the Christian Life, Notre Dame, Indiana: Ave Maria, 1974.

Reaching Out: The Three Movements of the Spiritual Life, Garden City, New York: Doubleday, 1975.

Genesee Diary: Report from a Trappist Monastery, Garden City, New York: Doubleday, 1976.

The Living Reminder: Service and Prayer in Memory of Jesus Christ, Seabury, 1977; New York: Harper and Row, 1981.

Clowning in Rome: Reflections on Solitude, Celibacy, Prayer, and Contemplation, Garden City, New York: Doubleday Image, 1979.

In Memoriam, Notre Dame, Indiana: Ave Maria, 1980.

The Way of the Heart: Desert Spirituality and Contemporary Ministry, Seabury, 1981; New York: Harper & Row, 1981.

Making All Things New: An Invitation to the Spiritual Life, New York: Harper & Row, 1981.

A Cry for Mercy: Prayers from the Genesee, Garden City, New York: Doubleday, 1981.

Compassion: A Reflection on the Christian Life, co-authored with Don McNeill and Douglas Morrison, Garden City, New York: Doubleday, 1982.

A Letter of Consolation, New York: Harper & Row, 1982.

Gracias! A Latin American Journal, New York: Harper & Row, 1983.

Love in a Fearful Land: A Guatemalan Story, Notre Dame, Indiana: Ave Maria, 1985.

Lifesigns: Intimacy, Fecundity, and Ecstasy in Christian Perspective, Garden City, New York: Doubleday, 1986.

Behold the Beauty of the Lord: Praying with Icons, Notre Dame, Indiana: Ave Maria, 1987.

The Road to Daybreak: A Spiritual Journey, Garden City, New York: Doubleday, 1988.

TAPES BY HENRI NOUWEN

A Spirituality of Waiting: Being Alert to God's Presence in Our Lives (Set of two) (1 hr. 24 min.)

Aging and Ministry (Set of two) (1 hr. 44 min.)

Desert Spirituality and Contemporary Ministry (Set of three) (2 hr. 58 min.)

Spirituality of Marriage and the Family (53 min.)

The Christ-Memory in Our Lives (39 min.)

For tape catalogues and price list write:

Ave Maria Press
Notre Dame, IN 46556

Also available on tape:

Prayer: The Way to a Transparent Life (38 min.)
With Outstretched Hands: Christian Leadership in the Future
   (Set of two) (2 hr. approx.)

Available from:

> Credence Cassettes
> P. O. Box 419491
> Kansas City, MO 64141

Index

"Adam's Story," 191ff
Advent, 101
Aging, 128, 130, 131
Alfrink, Cardinal Bernard, xix
Allport, Gordon, xxiii
Alpatov, M., 114
Amsterdam, xxi
Andre, Pere de Jaer, xxvi
"Apocalypse Now," 156
Armero, 156
Arms race (*See* Nuclear)
Augustine, St., 69
Auschwitz, 80
Autumn, 99

Bamberger, John Eudes, xxiv,
    xxxii, xxxiii, 41, 148
Basil, St., 146
"Beethoven Factor," 186
Bentley, James, 144, 145, 146
Bible (*See* Scripture)
Birds, 25
Body, human, dignity of,
    116–119, 147
  of Christ (*See* Jesus Christ)
Bonhoeffer, Dietrich, 74
Burns, Tom, 85

Bussum, Holland, xxi

California, 116–118
Call (God's), xxix, 69, 90, 93–95
Cancer, A personal story, 138,
    139
Care and Cure, 129, 130 (*See also*
    Aging, Compassion)
Career, 94, 95
Catharine's, St., Monastery (Mt.
    Sinai), 145
Chesterton, G.K., 82
Children, 31–34, 101
Christ (*See* Jesus Christ)
Christianity, 56, 57
Christmas, 108, 109
Chuang Tzu, 10
Codex Sinaiticus, 144, 145
Collegeville, MN, xxiv
Colombia (So. Amer.), 156
Community
  and peacemaking, 176
  and prayer, 80, 81, 90, 105,
    106
Compassion (*See also* Care,
    Aging)
  God's, 91

Compassion (*continued*)
  prayer and, 72, 73, 80
  Story of Old Man and
      Scorpion, 124, 125
Confessions of St. Augustine, 69
Conversion, 93
Crozier Fathers, xxi
Cupitt, Don, 146

Daybreak, xxvii, 192, 193, 201,
    203
Death, 132–137
Desert Fathers, 10, 60
Discipleship, 66, 91, 93
Displacement, 90–93

Ecstasy (In a Nuclear Age), 164,
    165, 187
Elizabeth (Luke, Ch. 1), 102–106
El Salvador, 169
Enemy love, 177–178
Eternity, 137
Eucharist, 100, 118, 121

Failure, 26
Faith, 43–46, 80
Forgiveness, 26, 27
Francis, St., of Assisi, 82, 83,
    168, 172, 187
Fraser, John, 153
Freud, Sigmund, 45, 46

Gandhi, 24, 161, 162
Genesee Abbey, xxiv, xxv,
    xxxii–xxxiii
Gilbert, Pere, 119, 120
Globe and Mail, 153

God
  absence of, 74, 75, 77, 78
  arguing with, 79, 80
  calls, xxix, 69, 89, 90, 93–95
  existence of, 50–52
  glory of, 126, 127, 148, 149
  presence of, 70, 71, 74–78,
      89, 91, 101
  seeing, 112–115
  silence of, 10, 11
Good Friday, 119–121
Gorbachev, Mikhail, 157
Grace, 63, 89
Gratitude, 89
  and peacemaking, 177
Gregorian University, xxiv
Gregory, St., of Nyssa, 146
Guatemala, xxxiv, 169

Handicapped (*See* "Adam's
    Story"), xxvi, xxvii, xxxiv,
    xxxv, 147
Harvard University, xxv, xxvi,
    xxvii
Heller, Bob, 144
Hesburgh, Father Theodore, xxiii
Heschel, Abraham, 79, 80
Hillman, James, 133
Hiroshima, 102, 171
Holiness (and Humanness), xvii–
    xviii, 39ff
Holland-American Line, xix
Holocaust, 169 (*See also*
    Auschwitz)
Honduras, xxv, xxvi, 203
Hope
  the cross, a sign of, 143
  a definition, xv
  and identity, xxxvii
  in a nuclear age (*See* Part IV,
      151ff), xix–xx

Hope (*continued*)
    three levels, xv–xx
    and waiting, 104
    word of, 102
Human Dignity, 100, 147 (*See also* "Adam's Story")

Icons, xxxiv, xxxv, 112–115
Ignatius, St., 63
Institute for Ecumenical and
    Cultural Research, xxiv
Intimacy, xxviii
Intimacy, 17–21, 57
Ireland, 134

"Jessie's Sparrow," 153
Jesus Christ, 77, 78, 88, 89,
    101, 102
    agony of, 122–124
    body of, 116–121, 145–147,
        186
    cross of, 119–121, 88, 143, 184
    eyes of, 112–115
    face of, 112, 113
    first peacemaker, 173
    glory of, 142–144
    hands and feet of, 126, 127
    passion and death of, 138–144
    resurrection of, 142, 144–147
    a revolutionary, 159, 160
    Second Coming of, 180–186
John Eudes (*See* Bamberger)
John, St., Klimakos, 146
John's, St., University, xxiv
Johnston, William, S.J., 150
Judgment, Last, 180–186

Koan, 148, 150

La Croix, 157
L'Arche, xxvi, xxvii, xxxiv–xxxv,
    147 (*See also* "Adam's
    Story")
Last Judgment (*See* Judgment)
Latin America, xxiv–xxvi, xxxiii,
    xxxiv, 83, 181, 185
Letter to Rhenigos, 146
Letter Writing, 29
Life, Celebrating, 35, 36
Loneliness, xxix, 12, 13
Lonergan, Bernard, 57, 58
Lord, "Who Is . . .?," 41, 42
Love
    nature of authentic—, 22–24
    possibility and desirability of,
        17

Magic (and Faith), 43–46
Malloy, Edward, 118
Mander, Jerry, 62
Mark, St., Gospel of, 146
Marriage, 20–22
Mary; Mother of Christ,
    102–106, 108, 110, 111
Maryknoll Mission Society, xxv,
    83, 84
Matthew, St., Gospel of, 183
Maximus, St., the Confessor,
    146
Meals, grace at, 63
Menninger Clinic, xxiii
Merton, Thomas, xxxi, 161–163
Message, problem of, 53, 54
Messenger
    authentic, 58–59
    perfect, 60
    problem of, 55–57
Michael's, St., College, Toronto,
    xxvi

Ministry, xxi, xxxi, xxxv, xxxvi
    challenge of, 53–61
    and God's absence, 77–78
    and God's presence, 76
McNeill, Donald P., 118, 150
Mysticism
    in a nuclear age, 159, 160

Negasaki, 171
Naq Hammadi, 146
National Catholic Reporter, xxviii
National Security, 164–167, 181,
    184
Nature, 99, 100
Nazis, xxi
Nicaragua, xxv, xxvi, 185
Nijkerk, Holland, xxi
Nijmegen University, xxiii
Nonviolence, 161–163 (*See* Part
    IV, 151ff.)
North American College, Rome,
    xxiv
Notre Dame University, xxiii,
    xxviii, xxx
Nouwen, Maria and Laurent,
    xxi, xxxii, 135–137
Nuclear war, (*See* Part IV,
    151ff.)
Nun, Story of Hypervigilant, 29–31

Obedience, xxix, 88, 89, 144

Pascal, Blaise, 123
Patience, 103
Peacemaking, 168–179, (*See also*
    "Adam's Story")
Phillipe, Pere Thomasa, xxvi,
    119, 120

Prayer
    and community, 80, 81
    and compassion, 68, 72
    in a busy world, 65
    and peacemaking, 172, 179
    and presence of God, 65, 70,
        75
    private, 80–81, (*See also* Silence
        and Solitude)
    problems of Westerners, 64
    of protest, 79
    and spiritual direction, 71, 72
    three rules, 69–72
    and TV, 62
    what is—?, 66–68
Prayers
    A Preacher's — , 61
    for a nuclear age, 188
    to Christ, 149
    to the God of Ebb and Flow,
        37
Porchia, Antonio, 151
Poverty, xxvii, 83ff., 202
Preaching, 53–61
Psalms, 75 (ps. 22), 99 (ps. 64),
    113 (ps. 139)

Rabbi, Story of, 204–205 (*See also*
    Heschel, Abraham)
Reaching Out, xxx
Reagan, Ronald, 157
Religion, 46–50 (*See also:* Faith,
    God)
Rembrandt, 130, 131, 157
Resurrection, 126, 142–147
Revolution, 159, 160
Rich, Larry, 85
Rother, Father Stanley, xxxiv
Rublev, Andrew, xxxiv, 112–115
    (*See also* Icons)

Ruggere, Pete, 85
Rumke, H.C., 45, 46

Sacraments, 100 (*See also*
    Eucharist; Jesus Christ;
    Marriage)
Santos, Dr. John, xxiii
Scotosis, 57, 58
Scripture, xxix, xxx, 69, 71, 72
Search for God, xxix, 47–50, 69
Secrets of Mount Sinai, 144
Sensuality, 118, 119
Sermon on Mount, 168
Sexual love, 23, 24
Shroud of Turin, 112
Silence, 6, 8–11, 70, 71
Solitude, 14–16, 70, 71
South America (*See* Latin
    America)
Spirit, 6, 7, 63, 77, 78,
    116–119, 135–137
Spiritual direction, 71, 72
Spiritual life, 4, 6, 105
Stoecklin, Pere Andre, 110
Stress in modern living, 6
Suffering, 122–124, 126,
    138–144
Suzuki, Shunryu, 132
Symbols of God, limitations, 49,
    50

Teaching religion, 47–49
Tischendorf, Von, Constantin,
    144, 145
Trappists, xxiv, xxxii, xxxiii

Trollope, Anthony, 53, 59
TV and prayer, 62

Utrecht, Holland, xxii

Van Gogh, Vincent, 37, 62
Vanier, Jean, xxvi, xxvii, xxxiv,
    147
    Madame, 153, 157
Vanstone, V. H., 139
Vesey, Father John, xxxiv, 30
Vietnam, 62
Virginia Theological Seminary,
    xxxv
Vladimir, Our Lady of, (*See*
    Icons)
Vocation, xxix, 94, 95

Waiting, 102–107, 140, 141
Wiesel, Elie, 96 (*See* pp. 79–80)
Williams, Colin, xxviii
Wilson, Ian, 112
Word of God, 11, 107 (*See also*
    Scripture)
Words and Silence, 8–11
Writing, 26–29
World War II, xxi, 168

Yale University, xxii–xxv, xxviii,
    xxxii, xxxiii, 83

Zechariah, 102–104

PRINTING HISTORY